Sol Gordon, Ph.D.

Judith Gordon, M.S.W.

Raising a Child Conservatively in a Sexually Permissive World

Revised and Updated

A Fireside Book

Published by SIMON & SCHUSTER, Inc.

New York

Copyright © 1983 by Sol and Judith Gordon
First Fireside Edition, 1986
Published by Simon & Schuster, Inc.
Simon & Schuster Building
Rockefeller Center
1230 Avenue of the Americas
New York, New York 10020
FIRESIDE and colophon are registered trademarks of
Simon & Schuster, Inc.
Designed by Karolina Harris
Manufactured in the United States of America

1 3 5 7 9 10 8 6 4 2 Pbk.

Library of Congress Cataloging-in-Publication Data
Gordon, Sol, date.
    Raising a child conservatively in a sexually
permissive world.

    "A Fireside book."
    Bibliography: p.
    Includes index.
    1. Sex instruction—Moral and ethical aspects.
2. Sex instruction—Religious aspects.   3. Parenting—
Moral and ethical aspects.   4. Parenting—Religious
aspects.   5. Parent and child.   I. Gordon, Judith,
1923-   . II. Title.
HQ31.G696   1986   649'.65   86-14323

ISBN: 0-671-62797-X Pbk.
The quotation on page 193 is from *Battered Women* by Lenore
E. Walker, © 1979 by Lenore E. Walker, reprinted by permission
of Harper & Row, Publishers, Inc.

Our book is dedicated to Bonnie, Gary and Michael Williams—an askable family.

Contents

	Introduction	9
One	The Family and the "Sexual Revolution"	13
Two	Promoting Self-Esteem in Children	22
Three	Coming to Terms With Our Sexuality	29
Four	Becoming an Askable Parent	42
Five	Sexuality Education in the Schools	55
Six	What Children Need to Know: The Preschool and Preteen Years	68
Seven	What Children Need to Know: The Adolescent Years	88
Eight	Parents' Questions About Adolescence	112
Nine	For Teenagers and Young Adults (and Their Parents)	144
Ten	STD—Sexually Transmitted Diseases	165
Eleven	Fostering a Child's Sexual Integrity in Special Situations	179
Twelve	The Family Is Alive and Getting Better	191
Thirteen	The Case for a Moral Sex Education	205
	Appendix A: Recommended Reading for Parents and Children Who Want to Know More	213
	Appendix B: Sources of Further Information	223
	Index	225

Introduction

This book is for parents who want to be the principal sex educators of their children, who want their children to grow up with healthy attitudes, and who are not apologetic about wanting to get across their own values. The book is written mainly to communicate that we are all born and remain sexual human beings, that nothing in life is definite, that even the best-intentioned parents make mistakes, that sex isn't everything (or even the main thing) in life, and that no book will change a person dramatically.

We write for parents who appreciate differing value systems, enjoy a sense of humor and try not to be hypocritical—in short, parents who would like their children to perceive them as understanding and "askable." Ultimately, the feelings of love and affection parents share and the atmosphere of caring in the home are more important to a child's healthy development than formal sex education.

Sex education begins in the home. Parents need to understand and facilitate the development of their children as sexual beings. While schools, religious groups and community agencies can assist, parents remain the primary educators. We hope this book will allay any fears parents may have that giving information to children will stimulate irresponsible or premature sexual experiences. The least respectable "authorities" on this subject are, in our judgment, those who claim, "If you tell kids about sex they'll do it," or "No one ever told me about sex, and I turned out perfectly all right." Knowledgeable and aware young people tend to develop healthier personalities and to be less exploitative of themselves and others.

Mature parents know that they have a responsibility to guide their children, and to exemplify the enduring values they cherish. They strive to put sexuality into perspective for their children and intuitively appreciate (as this book will make explicit) that of the ten most important aspects of a relationship, sex probably ranks ninth.

The reader is entitled at the beginning to know our basic philosophy. We don't believe that teenagers should engage in sexual intercourse—they are too young, too vulnerable and too available for exploitation. We consider teenage sexual intercourse to be a health hazard, both physically and emotionally. We further support strengthening family life by encouraging honest communication between spouses and between parents and children.

There are important distinctions to be made between sex and *sexuality*. Sexuality is what we're about in terms of love and intimate relationships, masculinity and femininity, feelings, values and attitudes. Sex, according to our usage, refers specifically to a range of sexual activities involving the genitals. We question whether this is the age of the sexual revolution in a positive sense, knowing that some of the most troubled people claim to be sexually "liberated." We support the notion of loving intimacy as the most important aspect of sexuality (indeed, much more important than orgasms). In order to be enlightened it isn't necessary to experiment with a variety of sexual experiences and lifestyles. We even think that adults can be happily married to and sexually gratified by one person all their lives (though we hope they will not be self-righteous about it).

We do not subscribe to the view that "if it feels good, do it," nor are we familiar with a single reputable sexuality educator in the country who endorses this somewhat popular misconception. Self-control is a critical dimension of responsible sexuality.

We do support the view that if parents are able to answer their children's questions about sexuality, it will be the opening for communicating with them about other crucial aspects of life. When you get right down to it, our book is about enhancing relationships between parents and their children.

CHAPTER ONE

The Family and the "Sexual Revolution"

W̲e as a society are good at discussing and declaring our morality, but we find it hard to face up to the consequences of our behavior. Most of us have lived through Watergate, the assassinations of the sixties and seventies, and Vietnam, and we are still witnessing the deterioration of our cities due to neglect and crime. Most of us—at least those who have not been directly victimized by these forces and events—have not been affected in our daily lives: we have moved away, accommodated, forgotten, repressed.

We are more preoccupied with our private lives—our families—and one of our chief concerns is protecting and enjoying our children. Yet one fourth of all our marriages end in divorce, and one half of all our teenagers engage in sexual intercourse before they graduate from high school. There are 1.3 million pregnancies each year among girls before their twentieth birthday, as well as several million new cases of venereal disease. Even if all recent surveys—*Redbook, Cosmopolitan, Playboy, Shere Hite*—as well as established scholarly research, could be discounted as exaggerated, there remains the accepted fact that the majority of men and women engage in premarital and/or extramarital sexual relations. The National Center for Health

Statistics reports that births to unwed mothers have reached an all-time high. The latest figures available indicate that from 1982 to 1983 the rate of such births increased by 3 percent. This amounts to 737,893 births to unmarried women.

Enough about hypocrisy. We, the authors of this book, are concerned about what is going on in the average American family. We have written this book not to save the world, but to convey a few basic messages. We want to help families who are trying to raise morally responsible children in this permissive world. We would like families to enjoy a sense of each other, parents to trust their children, and children to confide in their parents.

It is common to read that our world has become a less safe place for children because of a "sexual revolution," a new morality whose main ethic is: "Everyone should be free from repression and should do his or her own thing," or, simply, "If it feels good, do it." It is in this environment that our children are growing up—not the one in which their parents were raised. It is a world we, as those parents, seem to have little control over, despite the wish to influence it in some substantive way. It is the same world we sexuality educators deplore, however much some people hold us responsible for having caused it all.

For starters, there's television. Perhaps you have tired of hearing about all the rape, violence and promiscuousness on prime time. Yet there is a challenge here we cannot ignore, stated recently by Benjamin Stein in *TV Guide*. Mr. Stein, a well-known social commentator, wrote: "There is not one show on television today that's set in the present and that's not science fiction that presents a woman with young children who is married, secure and happy."*

Our children are further influenced by peer group pressure, fashions, sexploitative commercials, rock music (do it, do it), alcohol and drugs, to say nothing of the current wave of trashy films geared explicitly to teenagers.

Parents are rightly concerned over what their role should be in all this. There are so many dilemmas along the way. Parents want their children to be happy and popular. They want to

* Happily in 1986 we can report two exceptions—*The Cosby Show* and *Family Ties*.

nourish their children, to see them have friends and function well in school. They want their children to be moral and responsible, yet not be regarded as weird or out of the mainstream of their peer group.

The ultimate question is: How are parents to respond individually to the criticism often made that most children these days are no longer reared, they are turned loose? How do "conservative parents" respond *in fact* to what appears to most people to be *in fact* a permissive society?

First, let us clarify what we mean by conservative parents. We are not talking about the political scene, which is confusing enough. Some people regard anyone who is against prayer in the schools or believes in choice on the abortion issue as a liberal. Well, that would make Senator Barry Goldwater a liberal— over his dead body, to be sure. Goldwater said recently—and we agree with his position—that he was "frankly sick and tired" of the political preachers across the country telling him as a citizen that if he wanted to be a moral person he must believe in a certain way. There are many people and organizations who have preempted the meaning not only of conservatism, but also of family, flag and God; their interpretations are not shared by most true conservatives, either politically or personally.

When we speak of conservative families we are broadly referring to families who love their country, who respect its Constitution and laws, however much they may disagree with them at times (whether Democrats, Republicans or even Libertarians), and who believe in God (while worshiping Him in many different ways). Conservative families favor gradual as opposed to revolutionary changes to improve society. Conservatives support private enterprise and are law-abiding. They know that life isn't fair, but expect laws to be so. They believe that the family unit is the central constituent of their society, yet they accept God's message that all human beings are worthy and precious, whatever their social status. Conservative families do not enjoy meddling in others' lives except when called upon to be helpful to them. They want to live in good neighborhoods and enjoy being good neighbors. They do not want to impose their religious or moral views on others, although they are glad to share their beliefs. Conservatives differ on a wide range of issues, such as nuclear proliferation and government spending, but they generally agree that our democratic system is the best alternative.

Conservative parents want sexuality education in the schools, provided that the teachers are well trained and respect their values. Most of us are opposed to censorship, and all of us are opposed to minors having access to pornography and being sexually exploited by anyone. And, finally, if conservatives could live according to their best aspirations, they would prefer to live and let live.

We expect that some people are not going to like this book, especially those who believe strongly in corporal punishment for children, and who view the establishment of a "Christian Republic" as the solution to the permissiveness around them. This book is about what parents can do to help guide their children and to raise them to be young adults with good self-esteem and sound values. We don't endorse repressiveness, rash judgments motivated by fear, or abolishing the separation of church and state as acceptable means to that end.

One of the major forces at odds with the permissiveness which besieges the family today is religion. Religious worship has itself undergone significant changes recently, and to some people a spiritual malaise has resulted. Yet for us, religion remains a positive force. We both come from families who for generations have held religious tradition to be a central part of family life. Despite the posturing and alarms of a few, religion is for us, as it is for many conservatives, a source of inner peace and strength rather than a self-righteous call to arms.

Parents understandably have a stake in wanting their children to adopt their own religious orientation. This is often the case in homes where children are raised to have good self-esteem, a healthy attitude toward their own sexuality, and trust in other people. Young people who receive from their parents the essential religious and moral messages concerning sexuality will tend to incorporate them into their sexual decision-making. Religion can also provide education and instruction in how to handle intimate relationships, as well as some of the more factual aspects of sexuality. Some churches and synagogues have already developed good programs in this area. But let us be realistic.

Most churches and synagogues are having a difficult time. They must compete for attention with the mass media, chiefly television. It has become standard in some circles to blame secular humanism for the decline of morality and spiritual observance. Our view is that organized religion must accept the responsibility for its failure to be attractive, especially to young people.

Ironically, God's gift of sexuality, including the physical and psychic pleasure it provides, has been the source of great anxiety and controversy. The association of sex with the Fall of Mankind, and the resulting burdens of sin and guilt, colors many people's attitudes toward their own sexuality. The human conscience has always wrestled with these moral issues.

For those who find little meaning in religion itself, sexuality has spiritual connotations that need not be identified with any religious denomination or persuasion. As Abraham Maslow points out in his book *Religious Values, and Peak Experiences,** "spiritual values do not need supernatural concepts to support them."

Some readers will suspect that while we claim to be conservative, our views concerning sexuality are hardly so. This is, of course, their privilege, but we ask our readers for a larger understanding. Sexuality is, after all, a sensitive subject, and an all-too-common reading of the conservative position implies an opposition to communicating about sexuality, either at home or in churches and schools. Some people, therefore, might feel that our advocacy of communication between parent and child disqualifies us as conservatives, or even that it indicts us as part of the permissive society we're concerned with. It is the quality of such communication that distinguishes us as conservative. What we advocate are mature, educational discussions which are mindful of morals and responsibility.

Even we were astonished by the response of our college students who were given the assignment of discussing two of our children's books with their parents—*Did the Sun Shine Before You Were Born?*, designed for children under six years of age, and *Girls Are Girls and Boys Are Boys—So What's the Difference?*, for children aged six to nine. We received reports from

* A Penguin publication, 1970.

over a thousand students: most of their parents, the majority of whom were college-educated, revealed that they would have been uncomfortable letting their children read these books at the appropriate ages. Some would have refused. Yet, most also admitted that they would allow the same appropriately aged children to read them *now*. The difference seemed largely a matter of being influenced by the events of the last ten to fifteen years.

Following are several excerpts from the students' projects:

Overall, I enjoyed doing this assignment. I was shocked that my parents felt so positively about it [the book]. Before undertaking this project, I felt that they would be totally against giving a book like this to small children.

Although they never utilized any kind of formal education with their children, both of my parents said that they would have felt comfortable using the book as a teaching aid, but that they would not want the book to be within reach of a young child. They felt that *Girls Are Girls* . . . must be read with an adult on hand, in order to explain, expand, discuss and answer any questions the child might have. My parents' reaction to the book surprised me. Because of my lack of formal sex education at home, I assumed the subject made them uncomfortable and was taboo.

My parents do not feel that this book is suitable for any age group. Both of them believe that sex education should not begin until puberty, and that this book would be superficial at that time.

The best part of this assignment was the fact that it gave me the opportunity to have a meaningful sex-oriented conversation with my parents. Not only did we discuss *Girls Are Girls* . . . but we also talked about such things as premarital sex, birth control and abortion. My parents were uncomfortable talking about these things, but said later they were glad we had—and wished we had started sooner.

The real benefit of this assignment for our students, despite initial apprehension, was that they felt enthusiastic about it afterward. Despite parental reservations, the books stimulated one of the few—if not the only—discussions the students had ever had with their parents about sexuality. The assignment served to underscore the statistic that less than 20 percent of parents ever have significant discussions with their children about sex (the typical one-shot mother–daughter talks about menstruation notwithstanding).

We'll get more into this later, but we do appreciate that sexuality is a difficult subject for many parents. Yet a bumper sticker sighted the other day makes great sense to us: "If you think education is costly, try ignorance." A recurring theme in this book is, don't operate on the assumption that young people know everything these days. Where are they getting their knowledge from? From parents? From the schools? From churches and synagogues? No, most of what young people know they get from one another and TV, and most of that is just plain and simply wrong.

Our other message states that parents are the principal sexuality educators of their children whether they like it or not, so they might as well do the best job they can. Conservative parents are, after all, *at odds* with our permissive society, this sexual revolution which we prefer to call the antisexual revolution, and whose chief characteristics are readily recognizable. They are:

1. People have sex first and then consider getting to know each other. More often than not it's too late; the relationship is finished the morning after. It's as if the old fairy tale of the frog and the Princess had been rewritten. The modern tale is: the Princess kisses the Prince, he turns into a frog and hops away.
2. There is failure to understand that people get hurt not because they don't know how to make love, but because they don't feel loved (read Masters and Johnson's book *The Pleasure Bond*).
3. People use sex as a test of love; e.g., "If you really love me, you'll have sex with me."
4. The worst, most violent, sexist, exploitative media offerings are often the most popular. Worse has already come to worse here, and we parents may have to set some good examples by being more selective in our children's media

consumption, especially television, perhaps even pulling the plug occasionally. Experience suggests that the more bored, passive, vulnerable and exploitable a child is, the more that child watches television.

5. Sexuality is equated with orgasms—that is, with physical pleasure and performance rather than with love and intimacy.

We like what the popular psychologist and author Sam Keen once said: "When our eros is limited to genital sexuality it becomes obsessive, and boring, and finally destructive." The so-called sexual revolution offers little comfort to millions of lonely, alienated, desperate people needing love but only "getting laid" or "scoring." Arthur Schlesinger, Jr., has suggested that if sexual repression failed to produce happiness in the nineteenth century, sexual liberation appears to have done little better in the twentieth.

Conservatives in general will applaud the *real* sexual revolution, when one's sex behavior is private, moral, responsible and pleasurable, and when people respect each other, and lovers love each other. It will come. The question is, what do conservative parents do in the meantime?

First, become involved. A large part of this book concerns the strengthening of family life by promoting self-esteem in children. High self-esteem is correlated with growing up in families where children feel loved, valued, and that they belong. This joyful, exasperating parental task is at the cutting edge of all we believe in and write about. It can require a lot of faith on the part of parents—faith, as suggested by psychologist David C. McClelland, that loving and believing in your children will promote maturity in the long run, even if some of their behavior is unacceptable in the short run; faith that eventually they'll learn to make their own way.

Secondly, don't pine for the good old days. It's tempting to forget that in the 1930s 25 percent of our work force was unemployed. That not long ago women and blacks couldn't vote. That only the elite went to college. And who, after all, wants to return to the irrational guilt, ignorance and dismal repression of Victorian morality?

A third step lies in recognizing that some progress has occurred. Generally speaking, parents today have the number of children they want, when they want them. Adult sex for pleasure, as opposed to sex for reproduction only, is an accepted part of life. Many physicians and health-care workers are now required to take courses in human sexuality as part of their training, something unheard of in professional schools only fifteen years ago. Women are making progress toward being accepted and treated as equals.

Parents need to determine within their own families what to overlook and what to emphasize. This book suggests that parents should not overlook the sexuality education of their children, because no one else can take their place. Keep in mind as you read ahead that telling children only "not to"—not to smoke, drink, get high, have sex, or stay out late—doesn't help much unless you can also lead them to discover how to feel good about themselves. In the final analysis parents should not undertake the sexual education of their children in order to exercise ultimate control over them. Parents who do are unlikely to succeed. Rather, include sexuality education as but one part of a good relationship with your children.

This is a practical book for parents. We're keenly aware of the other problems relating to discipline of children, such as drug and alcohol abuse, performance in school, etc., even as we address just one specific, albeit essential, aspect of child rearing. Any book that attempts, in effect, to solve all such problems will wind up solving none of them. As the English ditty puts it: "One thing at a time and that done well / Is a very good rule as many can tell."

Nonetheless, parents who communicate with their children about the crucial topic of sexuality usually find that other areas of their relationship with their children improve as well. Psychiatrist M. Scott Peck has written, "When we desire to encourage the growth of the human spirit, we challenge and encourage the human capacity to solve problems. . . . It is through the pain of confronting and resolving problems that we learn." And without the promotion of self-esteem in children, efforts in none of these areas are likely to succeed.

CHAPTER TWO

Promoting Self-Esteem in Children

*P*arents have the right, indeed the responsibility, to demand certain behaviors of their children, such as honesty in relationships and being trustworthy, and to forbid others, such as drugs and stealing. Yet parents must be able to distinguish between their children's behavior and the children themselves. Let's explain that. Suppose a child behaves in a way that has been forbidden—tells a lie, denying that he broke the lamp in the living room. It is crucial for parents, at the same time as they enforce appropriate discipline, not to withdraw their love or reject the child. If the child is scolded, he or she must feel that, despite the transgression, he or she is still loved and valued. The behavior itself may be bad, but the child's own sense of worth and acceptance needs to be maintained. If the parents withhold love as a punishment, the child will come to feel unloved, and unlovable. As Anne Bernstein, a well-known psychologist, has written, "Children will come to value themselves as they have been valued by the significant people in their lives: treated with respect, they will respect themselves and be respectful to others in their turn."

Let's begin with the assumption that almost all parents mean well, don't have to be perfect and can afford to make mistakes. Children appreciate it when parents acknowledge their difficulties; an implicit theme of this book is, "If you make mistakes, turn them into lessons," or even "There are no mistakes—only lessons."

What is self-esteem? As a kind of pragmatic answer, we'd suggest that a person with high levels of self-esteem has the following traits. He or she:

- feels good about himself/herself;
- harbors a basic sense of trust in the self and others;
- doesn't exploit anyone;
- gets along in the family;
- has a sense of humor, and not at others' expense;
- forms relationships that are mutually enhancing;
- cares about other people's welfare.

A basic sense of *altruism* operates within people who feel secure enough in themselves to extend help, consideration and respect to others. Philosopher Robert Nozick has spent his lifetime evolving a concept of the good person's development. He writes:

> The developed person will want to help perfect others; this is the most important aid he can give them. We want to find a way of living whereby our best energies and talents are poured out so as to speak to and improve the best energies and talents of others. We want to utilize our highest parts and energies in a way that helps others to flourish.*

This area of altruism has also been explored by Erich Fromm and Erik Erikson, among others. Viktor Frankl believes that life isn't worthwhile unless the individual possesses a sense of purpose and meaning. Hans Selye, in his pioneering work in the area of stress, found that altruism is the most significant way for people to cope with and ease the levels of stress in their daily lives. So self-esteem is not just a matter of feeling good about oneself.

Yet feeling good about the self is the foundation of the kind of exemplary adulthood we describe—and that foundation is laid in childhood, in the bedrock of good parenting. A sense of basic trust is imparted in infancy itself.

---

* Robert Nozick, *Philosophical Explanations* (Cambridge, MA: The Belknap Press of Harvard University Press, 1981), p. 513.

A GOOD START

Generally, experts in the field of child development don't believe that it is possible to "spoil" a child in the first year of life. Parents sometimes worry that their baby will become spoiled if picked up or fed frequently, or if they respond quickly when the child cries. They fear that responsiveness will cause the child to become demanding, and to expect the same intensive attention when older. In short, parents fear that their children will become dependent and clinging. Interestingly, the opposite is usually the case. Parents who respond quickly to their crying infants and in other ways make the children feel secure will find their children becoming more *independent*. Specialists write that such children are "securely attached" to their parents; confident of their parents' love and care, they feel secure enough to explore the environment and develop their own skills.

During the first twelve months of life, then, it is better to err on the side of excess cuddling and responsiveness than on the side of minimal play and involvement with the child. This does not involve smothering the child. A prime parental challenge is not to adopt an overly rigid stance in relation to any of a child's behaviors or emotions. This crucial concept applies from birth through the child's lifetime.

In toilet-training a child, for instance, it is best to be both gentle and flexible in one's approach, and to maintain a healthy respect for the child's individual abilities and readiness. Weaning as well should not be harsh or abrupt and should proceed with sensitivity to the child's psychic and physical development. Researchers have found that when this "style" of parenting is combined with warmth and nurturance toward the child there is a greater probability that the child will in time display more comfort with all bodily processes, sexual and otherwise. There is also a greater likelihood that the child will possess confidence, good self-esteem and an important sense of self-acceptance.

As their babies grow into curious toddlers, parents can help foster self-esteem by praising and rewarding their children for doing well. More than anything else, this helps instill a feeling of competence. Competence breeds faith in oneself and one's body, a belief that the world is essentially safe, and trust in other people. It also provides the child with a sense of flexibility. Children who feel competent are resilient and can bounce back from inevitable failures and disappointments, secure in the knowledge that things will work out.

An issue of great concern, therefore, is that some parents interact with their children primarily around troublesome, negative situations. For example, children may be responded to mainly when they are crying, have done something wrong, are physically injured, and so on; at the same time, many seemingly minor accomplishments may be overlooked. Saying "Good job!" or giving a hug when a child finishes a puzzle or negotiates a steep set of stairs reinforces the child's sense of competence and self-acceptance. Parents also need to actively structure positive learning experiences for their children. Teach your child to tell time, build a sand castle, tie shoes, and perform some household tasks. Join in, participate and have fun with your child—but don't wind up taking charge completely. When parents merely demonstrate for their children how to do things, the children don't get the opportunity to do for themselves. In addition, they may be left with the impression that they can never master the task as well as Mommy or Daddy does. They may also be left with a residual sense that their bodies don't work well or are somehow "wrong."

As children become verbal and start spending time with other children, it becomes especially important for them to build competence in tasks which benefit other people. Without becoming capable of being helpful to others, children may feel themselves to be of little worth. Learning how to act altruistically, and modeling similar behavior of their parents, gives most children an important sense of purpose, which will serve them well in later life. This concept has been brilliantly elucidated by Swedish sociologist Benny Henriksson in his statement "Never before in our history and in no other cultures has it happened that people can reach the age of twenty-five without having learned to carry out a task which others benefit from or have use for, or without learning to take care of anyone who is old, sick, or small."

Equally important to parents is the principle of respecting

the unconscious instincts and emotions of the child. Parents can impose controls and make demands gently, according to the individual child's growing ability to exercise responsibility and restraint. By not enforcing demands according to an arbitrary schedule of child development, they can enhance the child's own sense of competence. Respecting the impulse life of the child also involves accepting as valid the child's feelings and experience of the world. For instance, children often have nightmares which frighten them and awaken them in the middle of the night. Parents hurry to their bedside with reassurances that "everything's all right," and "there's nothing to worry about." Though well-intentioned, such advice tends to invalidate the child's feelings. A much better response would be, "Yes, nightmares are troublesome, and many people have them. You'll find when you wake up that the bad dream disappears. You can tell us about the dream and we'll help you understand it."

Using this model, parents can enhance the child's understanding of him- or herself. Note that we are not encouraging impulsiveness in the child or a permissive attitude on the part of parents. We are saying that children's self-acceptance is bolstered when parents also accept parts of the child which may be thought of as frightening, negative or regressive. This helps to create an atmosphere in which a wide variety of subjects is open for discussion within the family. Parents and children don't have to discuss everything—in fact, a certain degree of room for private thoughts and feelings is desirable. But this ability to communicate remains an option, especially in times of stress.

In a highly recommended book, *Your Child's Self-Esteem*, Dorothy Corkille Briggs describes the inner dialogue of a child with low self-esteem: "I'm not very important. People wouldn't like me if they really knew me. I can't do things as well as others. There's not much point in my trying anything new because I know before I try that I'll fail. I can't make good decisions. I don't talk in groups because I don't say anything worth listening to. I don't like to go to new places. I hate being alone; in fact, I just wish I were someone else."

In our many years of counseling people of all ages, we have witnessed countless times how such low self-esteem leaves people open to being exploited, sexually and otherwise. With such low opinions of themselves, such individuals believe themselves deserving of poor treatment; even a poor relationship is better than none, and a little caring mixed with much abuse for them is better than no caring at all. Promiscuous and exploitative sexual behavior, premature parenthood and a range of self-damaging behaviors feed off poor self-esteem.

Among people with high self-acceptance, being taken advantage of is much less likely: one's self-worth dictates that most behaviors should be in one's best interests, constructive in nature. Conservative sexual behavior in this context means that it is wisely considered, premeditated and planned for, and in harmony with the person's values. Conversely, people who don't like themselves expect to be treated according to their own evaluation—that is, poorly. They don't value their own bodies or feelings and may overly value those of other people. In this way, others are seen as good, while the self is bad and usually to blame for anything that goes wrong.

Letty Cottin Pogrebin states this in another way in her book *Growing Up Free*. She writes: "Long-term studies have found that people who are most satisfied with their bodies tend to have the most confidence, self-esteem, and satisfying sex lives."

THE MORAL ISSUE

In the often conflictual and emotional area of sexuality, young people, like persons of any age, can be oblivious to consequences. Here the moral dimensions of behavior and decision-making assume great importance. The child's identity is closely related to the types of decisions he or she characteristically makes, and children with good self-esteem tend to resolve problem situations in ways which benefit the self (and which enhance the growth of others).

Within the boundaries of these moral considerations, there is reasonable latitude for the expression of individuality. Nevertheless, parents need to draw the distinction between acceptable personal styles of moral behavior and those behaviors which are almost never acceptable. For example, there will be days on which your sixteen-year-old son may be ill-tempered and short with his girlfriend; this kind of behavior is expectable occasionally. It can be tolerated if balanced by friendliness, courtesy and caring the rest of the time. But for your son to pressure his girlfriend to have sexual intercourse, with little regard for her feelings or no thoughts of contraception, is never acceptable behavior.

Moral considerations enter into political and societal forums as well. To illustrate: equality of the sexes, dignity and respect for all human beings regardless of their race, religion, sexual orientation or country of origin all stem from the fundamental democratic premise of equality. Equality does not always mean equal, or require the identical treatment for all people all the time. People simply aren't that good or consistent. What is involved is a *striving* to be moral, despite occasional mistakes and setbacks.

Good self-esteem is the cornerstone of sensible, moral decision-making, and ensures that people will not distort moral guidelines to suit their needs. Initiating a dialogue with one's children about moral issues, early in life, is necessary if they are to develop an understanding of morality. Such communication needs to convey the reasons why the values are important; parents who impose values with the rationale of "because I say so" will not usually find their children respecting these dogmatic beliefs.

Much has been written about self-acceptance in recent years, from "I'm Okay—You're Okay" to dozens of other books and articles. Though it is one of the simplest principles in psychology, it is also one of the most profound. In closing this chapter, we'd like to quote James B. Nelson's thoughts on self-acceptance, from his book *Embodiment*:

> Genuine self-acceptance is basic to humility. Authentic humility is not self-deprecation. It is realistic self-appreciation founded upon the experiential conviction of divine acceptance. It is the security of self that does not compulsively demand narcissistic support and constant affirmation from others. In contrast, self-rejection feeds upon illusions about the self's competence and virtue, often manifesting a need to be universally loved and admired. But such illusions mask a curious combination of arrogance and self-hate, pretense and anger.

CHAPTER THREE

Coming to Terms
With Our Sexuality

A strange alliance of forces in our society has "conspired" to debase the meaning, intent and value of sex. We know of well-intentioned ministers who claim that if you have sex before marriage you'll have nothing to look forward to in marriage or there will be no surprises after you marry. We suggest if you are expecting sexual intercourse to be the main surprise in marriage, don't marry. It's not worth it. Supersophisticated researchers would have us believe that sex is something you can "quantify," all of which contributes to the disastrous illusion that sex is akin to a gymnastic performance. Some researchers actually want us to take seriously the absurd notion that men reach their sexual peak at age nineteen and women at twenty-nine. Where did they get data like these? A distraught young man once came to us and remarked, "I'm twenty years old and already past my prime, and I haven't even started yet."

Most couples, when asked by researchers about the frequency of their sexual relations, tell an embarrassed lie. The statisticians add up all the lies and come up with an average of 2.2 sexual interludes a week. Why should it matter how many times a week a couple have sexual intercourse? The fact is that there are happily married couples who have sexual relations less than once a month and unhappily married couples who engage in sexual intercourse every day. As far as we can determine, there is no connection between the frequency of sexual intercourse and happiness or mental health. Nor are we impressed with the theorizing of a certain analyst who declared in a recent book that hostility was the "major force in enhancing sexual excitement."

We have often felt that many if not most studies in the area of human sexuality are based on a series of false assumptions—carefully documented by research. We may well ask, where is privacy? Where is love? Where is individuality? We are not against research, but we are for the rights of people—especially the right not to compare oneself with anyone else's "norm." We want to put sex into perspective. We see sexual intercourse as one aspect of a relationship; important, but not overwhelmingly so. In fact, sexual intercourse is, at best, number nine on our list of the ten most important characteristics of a mature marriage:

1. Love, sensitivity and respect for each other.
2. Honest communication.
3. Private thoughts and experiences.
4. A conscious sense of the essential equality of the relationship.
5. A sense of humor and playfulness, even about occasional "failures."
6. Adventuresomeness (physical and verbal), which includes displays of affection for each other.
7. Respect for "Don't feel like it."
8. Ability to enjoy foreplay and "afterglow" as well as:
9. Sexual intercourse.
10. Sharing responsibilities, including household tasks.

Occasionally, when we present this list to an audience, an outraged male suggests that we are talking nonsense—how could sex be number nine? Our reply is, "Because there are eight things more important. And, besides, of the 3,243 really important aspects of a relationship, sex is one of the top ten. Not bad."

It didn't surprise us when Shere Hite (in *The Hite Report*) found that most women she interviewed enjoyed hugging, kissing, cuddling, closeness and conversation as much as sexual intercourse. Overall, intimacy was more important than orgasm.

It is understandable and no cause for embarrassment that many parents are threatened by certain topics; few people reach adulthood without some areas of inhibition or difficulty. Parents do well to examine these areas realistically. The feeling of being uncomfortable may not disappear. But if parents are able to acknowledge their discomfort when discussing a sensitive subject with a child, they can help the child deal with his or her own feelings. Otherwise, children sense by the parent's words or mood that this is an area filled with anxiety and guilt, and that it is better not to discuss it.

Acknowledging an occasional vulnerability to one's children also casts the parent in a more realistic light; the aura of perfection which the parent may try to maintain can place impossible demands on the child, who realizes that he or she can't be perfect. Thus nothing the child does is ever good enough, and self-esteem sinks even further.

It is in this context that we shall now elaborate on some crucial aspects of sexuality—as an aid in helping you explore and evaluate your own sexual behavior, knowledge and feelings. This represents our judgment based on thirty years of study, research, counseling and teaching. We add to that our bias for common sense and respect for individual differences in preference to what is called "hard data." We present here twenty concepts, in no particular order.

1. *Normal and abnormal.* Normal sexual behavior among *adults* is defined by its being voluntary, nonexploitative and consensual. Generally, this behavior not only is pleasurable and guilt-free but also enhances self-esteem.

People tend to classify anything they don't approve of as abnormal, immature or immoral. Yet sexual behavior is abnormal only when it is compulsive (involuntary), exploitative, (often) nonconsensual, guilt-ridden and rarely pleasurable. It generally lowers self-esteem. More often than not it is a "defense" against feelings of depression or inferiority of which the person may not even be aware. Sometimes it is an act of violence, as in the case of rape. Provided sex is private, voluntary, enjoyable, and does not seriously conflict with the participants' values, it doesn't matter how and where it takes place—nor does it matter who does what.

2. *Sexual preference.* No sensible person need worry that heterosexuality as a primary lifestyle will disappear. The real concern in most of the world is overpopulation, not the presumption that more people these days are bi-, auto- or homosexual—or simply don't want to have children.

A person's basic sexual orientation is probably determined by the age of five years. This is the position of most respected scholars in the field. Yet it also seems evident that one's sexuality is not rigidly fixed. People can go through stages of sexual preference at different times of their lives.

3. *All thoughts are normal.* Sexual thoughts, wishes, dreams and daydreams are normal. No matter how "far out," they cannot, in themselves, hurt you. *Guilt is the energy for the repetition of fantasies that are unacceptable to you.*

Almost anybody with some degree of imagination has, from time to time, fantasies of murder, sadism, incest or rape. That does not mean you are going to act them out. As a matter of fact, accepting one's "unacceptable" thoughts as normal is the best way of keeping them under voluntary control. People who constantly repress their fantasies or become preoccupied with them because of guilt are the ones most likely to be harmful to themselves and others.

Here are two examples. A man walks down the street and notices a woman who captures his fancy. He thinks about having an affair with her. The woman doesn't know about it, his wife doesn't know about it, and he enjoys his walk. The sexual imagery is part of a huge, well-developed repertoire of fantasies.

A fifteen-year-old boy catches a glimpse of his thirteen-year-old sister taking a shower. The first thought that comes into his mind is to have sexual intercourse with her. He feels terribly guilty and cannot free his mind from the image or the sexual wish. Nobody in his family understands why he begins avoiding his friends, becomes hostile to his sister and gets more and more depressed. The fantasy becomes an obsessive, involuntary repetition of ideas. After a while he forgets (represses) the incident, and only the hostility to his sister remains. If this fellow only understood that his wish was normal, it would have remained with him for a brief duration (whether he enjoyed it or not doesn't matter) and nothing would have happened.

There are two kinds of guilt: *mature* and *immature*. Mature guilt is a response to something you did wrong. It helps people organize themselves and allows them to respond more rationally to similar future situations. Mature guilt can help you feel better about yourself. Immature guilt, on the other hand, saps your energy; it disorganizes and overwhelms you. You can usually tell if your guilt is immature if it is an *overreaction,* either to something you did wrong or, more commonly, to something you just thought about. More often than not it is a way of expressing hostility toward yourself and it results in feelings of depression. Almost everyone at some time or other suffers from immature guilt.

Most people have sexual thoughts when they are masturbating, having sexual intercourse and at other, sometimes less convenient times. *Almost* all reasonably healthy people *at times* find their fantasies more exciting than reality. As long as the fantasies are not accompanied by guilt, it doesn't matter what they are. Obsessions are harmful—not fleeting thoughts.

4. *Sexual arousal.* Popular culture, especially the mass media, creates the notion that there are standard stimuli for getting aroused. Men, for example, are supposed to be aroused by the "pretty girl" selling automobiles or by *Playboy's* bunnies. That's all right except that men who aren't aroused by current fashions of beauty often feel compelled to fake it. The fact is that human beings are sexually aroused by an endless variety of stimuli! *Not* knowing that *all* forms of arousal are all right is what causes trouble. The problem is somewhat more acute with men only because they can't always hide obvious erections.

Some people feel guilty if they are sexually aroused when playing with children, roughing it with dogs, being attracted to their parents, sitting in moving vehicles, having sadistic fantasies or looking at erotica. If one can accept the arousal experience without guilt, no harm is done. A problem exists if you can get excited only or mainly by thoughts or acts which you or your partner find unacceptable or exploitative.

To most sober people, bans on pornography constitute political weapons that threaten a resurgence of the days when even authors such as James Joyce and D. H. Lawrence were considered obscene. Right now some individuals and organizations want to ban J. D. Salinger's *Catcher in the Rye* from public and school libraries. Museums have been threatened with withdrawal of support if they don't discontinue allegedly "obscene" exhibits.

We know from literally hundreds of studies that even "hardcore" material designed entirely to appeal to our so-called "base instincts" is usually not harmful. In fact, pornography seems to help some people contain their potentially dangerous sexual impulses, and many teenagers have a natural curiosity about it. Usually it represents a passing phase, but if pornography becomes their main understanding of sex it can have a harmful effect. With the increasing proliferation of hard-core pornography, it is all the more important that parents provide the opportunities for accurate information and open discussion about sex.

5. *Women's liberation.* Some people have come to associate the women's-liberation movement only with issues such as abortion on demand, day care and assertive behavior, but liberation is much more than this. Liberation means that you are attempting to discover yourself in a realistic rather than idealistic or culturally stereotyped manner, and then *acting* on your discoveries. Explaining these new feelings and actions is one of the most important bridges that men and women must build.

6. *Masturbation.* Nearly all professionals these days say that masturbation is all right. Then there is a pause—"It's all right if you don't do it too much." And nearly everyone is asking the question "How much is too much?"

Masturbation is a normal sexual expression for all people, no matter at what age or stage in life they happen to be—child, teenager, young adult, middle-aged, elderly, single or married.

Masturbation causes no physical harm, no matter how frequently it is performed. Men need not worry that their sperm supply is affected, nor that they are expending "energy" necessary for sports or other enterprises. A wet dream (nocturnal emission in males) and orgasm stimulated by dreams in women are as natural as any form of sexual expression.

The idea that people who masturbate "a lot" (what's a lot?)

don't make friends or are selfish is just plain silly. Eating, talking, sleeping and masturbating are examples of "natural" behavior which can be compulsive, and thus symptomatic of problems. This does not make eating, talking, sleeping and masturbating "unnatural." If we had to "select" the least harmful
compulsive behavior to express our problems we would certainly
choose masturbation.

Though they seldom admit it, some men and women achieve
their best orgasms by masturbating. A lot of married people with
satisfactory sex lives also masturbate. Some people masturbate
hardly at all or not at all, and that's all right, too. Guilt about
masturbation is about the only thing that's not desirable.

7. *Telling the truth about your sexual past.* This may be a
good thing, but you should make sure that you are telling the
truth for the right reasons. Sometimes people reveal "the past"
in order to hurt or express hostility toward their partners.
Others want to know the past for ulterior purposes. It is not a
sign of love to "let it all hang out." We are all entitled to privacy
in some aspects of our lives.

8. *Coitus.* Many myths are perpetuated by "sexperts." There
is no special amount of time a man's penis is supposed to stay
in a woman's vagina in order to guarantee satisfaction. For
some, it's thirty seconds; for others, a couple of minutes; it can
even vary from time to time. The presumed norm of fifteen
minutes is ridiculous; many couples find this amount of time
too long. There are no standards for everyone or even almost
everyone. Each couple must discover what is most enjoyable for
them.

Intercourse is not essential for sexual pleasure—nor is having
an orgasm each time or even most of the time, and certainly not
having simultaneous orgasms. There are many ways couples can
enjoy sex. Mutual pleasuring and/or masturbation are alternatives. The largest number of uptight people are found among
heterosexuals who do "it" only one way—in the so-called "missionary position." Any relentlessly fixed sexuality is at best un-
imaginative.

9. *Female orgasms.* More nonsense has been written about
this subject than about any other area of sexuality. Women
have been made to feel so insecure that some need a *Good*

Housekeeping Seal to certify their orgasms. Often they pose the question in a serious way to a professional: "How can I tell if I have an orgasm?" And just as often the professional will respond with an idiotic answer like "If you had one, you'd know it." This response only reinforces a woman's insecurity.

Orgasm is mainly a psychological phenomenon—with associated physical sensations. We define orgasm as a very brief, intensely pleasurable sensual experience accompanied by a series of genital contractions. Orgasm is not always necessary in order to enjoy sexual intimacy.

Most women who enjoy their own bodies, who have good feelings about themselves and who like the idea of sexual intimacy have orgasms

- if they are not intent on having one each time.
- if their partner doesn't ask each time, "Did you have one?" (What kind of conversation is that, anyway?)
- if they feel comfortable about masturbating.

Male orgasms. The best-kept male secret is the myth that every time a male ejaculates he has an orgasm. This simply is not true. Any man who denies it either is not telling the truth or can't be trusted. Sometimes a man will ejaculate and feel nothing at all. At times there is a little pleasure and at times a great deal. Orgasms vary in strength and pleasure. We suspect that men sometimes fake orgasms. Male orgasm is just as much a psychological phenomenon as is the female orgasm.

10. *Size of genitals and breasts.*

Penis. An all-American hang-up! Men worry whether theirs is BIG enough. Have any of you males noticed men looking around in public bathrooms or showers to see if they can find one smaller than their own? Freud got it wrong. It's *men* who have penis envy. Size has nothing to do with giving or receiving sexual pleasure. What's more, one cannot tell the size of a penis by looking at it when it is not erect. Some that appear quite small will erect to sizes larger than those that appear huge in the flaccid state.

Vagina. Women needlessly worry that their partner's penis is either too small for satisfaction or too big ("painful") for their "small" vagina. When we recall that the vagina accommodates the birth of a baby, it is not difficult to appreciate that genital size itself is not a factor in pleasure or pain.

Breasts. Breast size or shape has nothing to do with sexual or personal adequacy. In the early stages of puberty, girls often worry because of uneven or late breast development in comparison to their friends.

Many females with large breasts are as self-conscious as those with small ones. The "style" of late has been: the larger the better. At other times, preferences dictated the smaller the better. Don't let style mess you up.

11. *Sublimation.* People used to think (and some still do) that one could sublimate sex—i.e., propel it into "higher channels" without direct expression—by being creative, athletic, doing charitable work or becoming a priest or a nun.

Adult sexuality can only be

- expressed,
- repressed or
- suppressed;
- it cannot be sublimated!

Individuals who repress their sexuality have a great potential for problems. Repressed sexuality is often revealed in the following ways:

- physical disorders
- immaturity
- revulsion in response to natural functions of the body
- meanness
- obsessive-compulsive neurosis
- fears of homosexuality
- failure to achieve orgasm
- a few other odds and ends

There are some emotionally mature people who choose to remain celibate. They are usually able to acknowledge, but suppress, impulses toward sexual relations or masturbation.

Many people who are emotionally immature have an active, vigorous sex life, as do many people who are emotionally mature. The range of sexual expression as it relates to maturity is infinite.

12. *Normal sex problems.* Just about everybody is sexually dysfunctional sometimes; in other words, they are unable to "perform" despite wishing they could. An occasional experience of impotence, premature ejaculation or lack of sexual desire is not uncommon. If you don't panic, the situation will improve. If you attach too much importance to what would otherwise be a temporary problem, it can get worse.

13. *Role playing (positions and techniques).* Sexual relationships thrive on variety. One partner can be active or passive, both can be active, or both passive. Just as one can care for someone or be taken care of, bathe someone or be bathed, massage or be massaged, one can play different roles. No one need be frozen in an assigned role. Traditional concepts of what is supposed to be male and female (or active and passive) no longer apply, if they ever really did.

What counts is communication and intimacy—sexual rapport. Roles, positions and techniques are only the mechanical how-tos in a loving, responsive relationship.

14. *Sexual desire.* Feeling horny is not mainly physiological, biological, constitutional or hereditary. It is primarily a psychological phenomenon. If you feel turned on and your spouse has a headache (which is lasting for days), consider masturbating. If you have a mature (not guilt-ridden) attitude toward self-pleasuring, you will feel better afterward.

15. *Homosexuality.* It is no longer believed that homosexuality is caused by any one thing or even by a special combination of factors. Homosexuals exist in every culture and society. Ancient Greek culture found homosexuality acceptable. Our culture has frowned upon it.

Homosexuality is not hereditary, biological, chemical or constitutional. We wonder sometimes how homophobia interferes with people's natural impulses. Men in our society can be especially frightened by normal desires for intimacy with other males because of their fear of being considered homosexual.

In any case, we now know that homosexual experiences are not rare during childhood and adolescence. These experiences do not necessarily mean that a person will be gay as an adult. One and even some homosexual experiences don't make a person homosexual any more than one or some heterosexual experiences make a person heterosexual.

It is a false assumption that a person who has homosexual thoughts or dreams must be a homosexual. Mature people are aware that they have both homosexual and heterosexual feelings, even though most prefer sexual activities with members of the opposite sex. In this connection, it might be helpful to point out that it is not easy to judge a person's sexual orientation by appearance. Some "feminine"-looking men or "masculine"-looking women are heterosexual, and some macho "all-American" types are homosexual.

People who are afraid of their healthy sexual impulses have a problem no matter what their sexual orientation.

Sexual orientation does not determine whether a person is mature or "normal." Saying that a person is a homosexual tells us as much about the person as saying that a person is a heterosexual.

People have the right, without stigma or coercion, to be what they are. If some 90 percent of the population are heterosexual, that's their business. If perhaps 10 percent express themselves by homosexual, bisexual or no overt sexual behavior, that's their business as well. The government has no right to have any say about sexual relations between two consenting adults.

We hope that there will come a time when people's sexual preferences will be of little or no legislative interest and certainly none of anybody's business (unless that body is an unwilling partner).

16. "*Perversion.*" This is an old-fashioned word often used to describe what some people find revolting. For example, there are people who consider anal or oral sex perverted. The word "perversion" is sometimes used to describe such deviant behavior as exhibitionism, masochism, sadism, fetishism, voyeurism, necrophilia and bestiality.

We think there is nothing wrong with any kind of sex between adults in private if each partner is nonexploitative and the act is voluntary. Anal and oral sex are enjoyable for many people and are also ways to have sexual pleasure for those who don't want to have sexual intercourse.

If we use the word "perversion" at all, it should be restricted to sexual behaviors which are harmful to another person. This refers to sexual activity which is usually compulsive and guilt-ridden. Examples might be a male who gets his kicks from displaying his penis in a public place or a woman who enjoys intercourse only when she causes physical pain to her partner.

We all have "perverted" feelings at times. They are neurotic and harmful only when they are translated into behavior, or obsessively repeated.

17. *Fear of other people's preferences.* It's all right to have sexual preferences. It is not necessary to enjoy or "be into" anal, oral, auto, homo or group sexuality in order to be "with it." Nevertheless, having fixed, powerful emotions of revulsion or disgust in response to behavior which is enjoyable *to others* means you have a problem.

18. *Immature, neurotic or immoral sex.* Sexual practices can be manifestations of immature or neurotic behavior. Here are four of the more common types:

- Compulsive masturbation. You do it not because you like to but because you can't help it.
- Compulsive heterosexual or homosexual behavior (even if not forced on the other person). This behavior takes place outside an interest in a relationship. It does not enhance or enrich the person and it rarely provides more than momentary relief. A person who is always "on the make" is rarely capable of a sustained relationship and, despite boasting to the contrary, usually does not enjoy sex.
- Excessive compliance. You can be talked into having sex when you really don't want to; before you feel ready for it; with someone you really don't care about; and without using birth control.
- Fetishism and other compulsions. Your main type of sexual outlet is to transfer your attachments to a thing (shoe, undergarment, dress); or you are compelled to expose yourself, steal, or secretly view others (voyeurism) as a form of sexual expression.

And here are the Seven Deadly Sins of immoral sex:

- Rape, molestation and sexual assault.
- Hurting, forcing, deceiving, exploiting, and corrupting.
- Sexually irresponsible behavior (such as a man abandoning a pregnant woman).
- Perpetuating the double standard.
- Sex stereotyping.
- Sexual harassment of women.
- Lying to young children about the facts of life.

19. *First experiences of sexual intercourse.* Many first experiences of sex are not pleasurable, despite stories to the contrary. This is especially true if you are too young, too immature or on your honeymoon.

It is especially important not to diagnose yourself on the basis of these experiences. Men think they are sexual freaks if they are impotent or ejaculate prematurely on their first encounters. Women feel that they are not sexual or feminine if they don't have an orgasm the first time around.

It is surprising how many people have acknowledged that their first sexual experiences were empty, flat, even repulsive.

20. *On being sexually attractive.* People who are self-accepting are sexually attractive to some other individuals, period. It doesn't matter what the cosmetic and toothpaste industries have to say about it.

It's not that short, fat or "unattractive" people can't find or hold a mate. Instead, people who hate themselves and express it in being (not looking) unattractive, shortsighted or fatuous tend to repel rather than attract others.

Believing that certain perfumes, hair tonics, vaginal sprays or selective techniques or positions will make you "attractive" will get you nowhere. Being an authentic person is what is attractive to other people.

In later chapters we shall be delving deeper into some of the important concepts presented here. However, we hope that this was a good way to introduce you to our basic orientation, and to help you examine your own attitudes about sexuality so that you may become a more askable parent.

CHAPTER FOUR

Becoming an Askable Parent

Although parents are expected to be the primary sexuality educators of their own children, survey after survey reveals that they often fail in the task. Even parents who think they have done a good job would be sadly surprised to hear the opinions of their children: "My parents? You must be kidding!" "I learned a little from my friends, only to find out after I left home that most of what I thought I knew was not true."

Let's try to put to rest two myths which are partly responsible for the ever-increasing incidence of irresponsible sexual behavior among the young.

The first myth is that today's young people already know everything there is to know about sex. Some do, of course, but research reveals a staggering ignorance about critical issues. In a recent Johns Hopkins University study of adolescent girls, it was found that 59 percent did not know when in the menstrual cycle the risk of conception was greatest. Worse, young people with little sexual experience will often feel compelled to exaggerate the extent of their activities.

Don't believe the stories that young people knowingly take risks, or that girls from disadvantaged homes deliberately try to get pregnant. Research on teenage pregnancy usually involves asking pregnant girls if they had originally wanted to conceive. In one such study of three hundred teenagers (in a *single* high school), we asked why the girls hadn't practiced birth control.

"Oh, but we did," was the general response.

"I used one of my mother's pills."

"I didn't think I could get pregnant standing up."

"He said he'd pull out in time."

"I didn't think I could get pregnant the first time."

When we asked three hundred sexually active but not yet pregnant girls if they wanted to get pregnant, a full 90 percent said they did not. A typical comment was, "Do you think I'm stupid? I'm only fourteen." Furthermore, in surveys of high-school students, more than 90 percent did not know that the original symptoms of venereal disease disappear after a while. Most assumed that the disappearance of the symptoms meant that the disease had been cured. A majority of the same students did not know that females generally have no symptoms at all when they are infected with gonorrhea.

Some readers may already be thinking that their own children are not involved in sexual experimentation. It should be remembered that whether anyone likes it or not (including the teenagers themselves), more than half of all high-school students will have had sexual intercourse before graduation.

Each year the Institute for Family Research and Education receives hundreds of poignant letters from teenagers. A number begin something like this: "I'm fifteen, pregnant, and I can't tell my folks (they'll kill me). What should I do?" More typical are those such as this one:

> I come from a family where I have learned sex from my friends. My mother don't mention it to me. And I still don't know what most of sex and love is all about. So I would like to know because I'm only 14 years of age. And I've seen my friends get pregnant. I'd like to know what it's all about. Thank you.

The 1.3 million teenage pregnancies in 1985, the 3 million new cases of sexually transmitted diseases (STDs) among persons under twenty-five in the same year—these documented tragic consequences of widespread misinformation belie the myth that young people "know it all."

The second myth is that knowledge is harmful. Virtually all opposition of sex education is based on the assumption that children who "know about sex" will practice it. Even editors of metropolitan newspapers often blame sex education for the rise of illegitimate births and venereal disease. Yet, as we will detail later, for the vast majority of American students sex education is simply absent from the curriculum.

Our research tells us that young people who do not understand "the facts of life" are more likely to make mistakes. In fact, well-informed young people are more likely to delay sexual experiences, at least until after they finish high school, and then to use effective contraception.

THE PARENT'S ROLE

Most parents, after all, want to educate their children about sexuality. They realize that schools, churches, community organizations and the mass media can offer only supplementary education at best and, in any case, cannot be expected to reflect their personal values. Many parents also fear that too much information too soon will overstimulate their children, will arouse otherwise dormant sex impulses. This attitude is the first of many roadblocks to effective sex education in the home.

Contrary to a few experts in this field, we've never been able to discover a documented case of a child's having been overstimulated by facts alone. Should parents err by offering too much information, children will simply get bored, turn them off or cut the conversation short with an unrelated question. Fear, unresolved curiosity and ignorance are far more likely to result in overstimulation than are facts, lovingly offered. Our campaign against ignorance has led some opponents of sex education to tell jokes about us. A popular example: a child asks where she came from, and her mother responds with an elaborate explanation of the seed and the egg. At the end, the amazed child explains that she only wanted to know if she came from Philadelphia. To this, our response is a giggle and a simple retort: "So what? Now the child knows not only where she was born but how she was born."

Quite understandably, many parents who did not receive sex education in their own homes feel uncomfortable talking about sexuality with their children. There is no instant remedy for such feelings, but it may be helpful to ask the question, Who is really comfortable about anything these days? Contrary to modern theory, it simply is not necessary to feel entirely comfortable about sexuality in order to communicate effectively with your children.

As the primary force in your child's life, you are providing sexuality education in one form or another no matter what you do. The question is not *whether* you will teach your children about sex, but *how well*. Silence teaches no less eloquently than speech. If you convey to a young child, or a teenager, the impression that you feel a bit awkward discussing love and sex, chances are good that you'll score. Your child might well respond to your honesty with affection and appreciation, with a hug and a kiss and verbal reassurances that your discomfort is perfectly understood. Many a parent has been happily surprised to hear a child say, "Don't worry, Mom! It's all right."

Parents who worry that they don't know enough about the subject to be effective teachers ought to pause and consider this question: How much is it really necessary to know? To a particularly technical or baffling question, a parent can always respond with the truth: "I don't know, but I'll look it up for you and tell you tomorrow." "Let's look it up together" would be an even better response. A small child's questions can usually be answered with a few words of elementary explanation. Older children are more likely to ask questions about values than about anatomy. Even so, with excellent books no more distant than your local library, what excuse do you really have for remaining silent?

It's popular these days to conceive of children growing up in "stages"—be they fashioned by Gesell, Freud, Kohlberg, Erikson or Piaget. Frankly, as interesting and as creative as these theories are, we rarely see real children progress in an orderly sequence. Children are full of surprises. Concepts that some intelligent children understand at three and four still baffle others at nine and ten (even when the measured IQs are similar). Parents who shun baby talk with their small children, but rather use the correct words, e.g. "vulva," "vagina" and "clitoris" instead of "thing" or "down there," etc., find that their children grow up with good vocabularies.

We are interested in this phenomenon because we often hear warnings about not giving children sexual information before their "stage" has arrived. We encourage parents not to worry about offering information before a child can wholly comprehend it. Haven't you noticed that complicated fairy tales are fascinating to children whether they understand them all or not? They'll simply get what they can, and the rest goes over their head—or into their unconscious. Either way, it's OK.

Use common sense but respond to all questions regardless of stage. Remember that children at different ages will often ask what you believe are questions already answered. "Where did I come from?" asked at age five is not the same question when posed at nine or ten. Some children will never ask questions regardless of the stage they're supposed to be in, and some will begin to ask highly abstract questions before they are supposed to be able to do so. Parents are far less likely to go "wrong" by responding to children's questions with perhaps a little more sophistication than they believe the child can handle, than they are by underestimating the child's capabilities.

Some parents are concerned about making honest mistakes or giving wrong answers. Parents should realize that they can make mistakes without harming their children. The following examples may be illustrative.

A child wanders into the bedroom while you and your spouse are having sexual intercourse. You tell the child, "Leave," then worry that you have been too harsh. In the morning you can apologize for not having said "Please leave." Then you can explain what you were doing. If your child asks to watch the next time, kindly but firmly explain that sex is private. A child may not understand the prohibition, but later in life he or she will grow to appreciate the concept of privacy. Most important, learn to laugh at the outrageous proposition that a child who has witnessed sexual intercourse will need years of analysis to get over it. The person who, as a child, never once saw his or her parents being naturally and openly affectionate is a more likely candidate for analysis.

Perhaps you are worried about your neighbors' response if your child were to tell the truth about sex to some friends. Their parents hear about it and inform you, in no uncertain terms, of their horror and indignation. We don't think you should be swayed by their attitudes. Your responsibility is to tell your children the truth without instructions to keep it confidential. If your neighbors don't like it, that's their problem. And remember, no matter what parents do, children will share whatever information they have about sex; it's about time that well-educated children become an important neighborhood resource with respect to sex education. We realize that your child may be deprived of a playmate, but in the long run this kind of sensitive experience could contribute to your child's being more creative, happier and better adjusted.

NINETEEN KEY QUESTIONS

Of the thousands of questions we get from parents, the following are the most common. It is not expected that you will agree with all our responses, which express our personal values.

► 1. *When should I tell?*

The answer is simple: It is time to tell whenever the child asks. If you are an askable parent, your child may come to you with questions about sex from the time he or she is two or three years old. Young children's questions are sometimes nonverbal. For example, a child may constantly follow you into the bathroom.

Some shy children might ask no questions at all, even of the most askable parents. If your child hasn't raised sexuality-oriented questions by the age of five, you should start the conversation. Read a book with your child. Tell him or her about a neighbor or a relative who is going to have a baby. While it's fine on occasion to make analogies to animals, do not concentrate on them in your explanations. People and animals have very different habits.

► 2. *How much should I tell?*

You should tell your child a *bit* more than you feel he or she can understand.

► *3. How explicit should I be?*

Make it a point to use the correct terminology. Avoid such childish expressions as "pee-pee" or "wee-wee." Say directly that when a husband and a wife love each other and want to have a baby, the man puts his penis into the woman's vagina. If the sperm from the man's body joins with the egg (or ovum) inside the woman's body at the right time, a baby gets started. Depending upon the child's age and other factors, you might say more: "Sometimes it takes a year or two before a child gets started." Or, "Your father [or mother] and I enjoy loving each other in this way. Right now we are using birth control because our family isn't ready for a new baby just yet."

The main idea is that parents can be explicit without overstating the case or feeling compelled to describe sexual relations to a child who hasn't yet grasped much more basic ideas. It is also wiser to say at the start that a baby has its beginning in the mother's uterus, not the stomach.

► *4. Is there such a thing as giving too much sex education too soon?*

Parents worry a great deal about whether they can "harm" their children with "too much" information or by telling their children things that they won't understand. Let us state again that despite the protests of a few experts, knowledge is not harmful. It does not matter if the child does not understand everything you say. What counts is that you are an askable parent. If the child can trust you not to be rigid or hostile in your response or to give misinformation, he or she will ask you questions and use you as a source of wisdom and guidance.

► *5. What about nudity in the home?*

Many parents are relaxed about undressing in front of young children or bathing with them. These are good opportunities for children to ask important questions: "How come you have one and I don't?" "How come yours is bigger than mine?" "How come you have two and I don't have any?" Parents should respond directly to these and similar questions.

A question also arises when a child wants to touch a parent's genitals or breasts. There are several acceptable responses, one of which is simply that you don't want him or her to do this.

Even if children protest against that familiar double standard—"But you touch me"—you can explain that this is because you have to bathe them and keep them clean. In any case, don't make a big thing out of it. A child's own growing sense of modesty will tell you when to start undressing in private. When a child wants to go to the bathroom alone or to undress without an audience, parents need to respect that developing sense of privacy.

► *6. Is too much masturbation harmful?*

Masturbation is a normal expression of sexuality at any age. Once this is clear to the child, he or she will not feel guilty and thus will be much less likely to become a compulsive masturbator. It is guilt that creates the energy for compulsive masturbation. That masturbation is a private activity needs to be made clear, and all children old enough to understand the concept of privacy can be taught this.

► *7. What about the use of obscenities?*

Children use vulgar language to find out what it means, to get a rise out of their parents or to test a new and powerful weapon. If a child uses an obscenity, the parent should quickly and calmly explain its meaning, perhaps using the word itself in the explanation. Even the most common four-letter word can be handled in this way, provided the parent explains its gross intent as well as the fact that it's a crude synonym for sexual intercourse. There is an advantage in using the obscenity itself in your explanation: thereafter the word can hardly be used by the child as a "weapon." Furthermore, your openness reinforces your role as an askable parent.

► *8. What about the child who likes to look at his father's*
Playboy magazines, or at the nude photographs that are
becoming more common in ordinary magazines?

There is no harm in this. In fact, it may provide an opportunity for teachable moments. You might point out that not all people look like that, and state simply that men sometimes like to look at nude photographs of women, and women sometimes enjoy looking at photographs of nude men. It's no big deal.

Hard-core pornography is something else again. Though it

has not been proven harmful, it is clearly not educational, and parents would understandably prefer to keep their children away from it. While it may not always be possible to shield a child from pornographic material, parents can take some comfort in the fact that people who have received enlightened sexuality education tend to grow bored with pornography quickly.

► 9. *What about embarrassing questions in public?*

Children have a great knack for asking the most delicate questions in the supermarket or when special guests have come to dinner. The best approach, no matter how embarrassed you are, is to tell the child that he or she has asked a very good question; if you still have your wits about you, proceed to answer it then and there. In most cases, your guests will silently applaud. If you feel you can't answer the question right away, it is very important to praise the child for asking, and to state specifically when you will discuss it. In general, it is better to risk shocking a few grown-ups than to scold or put off your own child.

► 10. *What should I do if my husband thinks it's my job to tell our child about sex?*

Sexuality education is properly the responsibility of both parents. It is reflected in their behavior with each other and in communication with children. If your husband refuses to have any part of it, you must take it upon yourself to explain sex and love to all the children in your family. Incidentally, it has never been established that girls are better educated by their mothers or boys by their fathers. Single parents, relax.

► 11. *What can I do to prevent my child from becoming a homosexual?*

Some parents have rather strange notions of what constitutes "protection." Contrary to the opinion of some professionals, our view is that there's nothing parents can do to prevent their children from becoming homosexual. No specific attitudes or behaviors have been found to discourage the development of a homosexual orientation. Similarly, there is no convincing evidence that parents can cause homosexuality in their children. It is important to understand that good mental health is not necessarily a function of sexual orientation. Just as homosexual adults can be happy and creative individuals, heterosexual adults can turn to drugs or crime and generally lead unhappy lives.

There are fathers who are reluctant to be affectionate with their sons after age five or six for fear that the child will become homosexual. This is unjustified and very distressing to the child. Some parents overreact to their children's play when it does not conform to long-standing stereotypes—for example, when boys play dress-up in women's clothing or play with dolls, or when girls play tough and like sports. Certain parents are even upset because their young sons like to read a lot! These are rarely signs that the child is growing up homosexual.

Parents should convey an attitude of acceptance for people who have different sexual orientations.

► *12. What if my children think I'm old-fashioned?*

They will probably be right! Most parents are old-fashioned. Acknowledge it and continue expressing your views without worrying which label your child might attach to them.

► *13. How can I talk to my teenage daughter about birth control without giving her the message that it's all right for her to have sexual intercourse?*

Some parents believe that teenagers equate information with consent. Your teenage children know very well what your values are. It's one thing to tell a daughter that you will disown her if she becomes pregnant; it's quite another to explain your feelings something like this: "We really think you're too young to have sexual intercourse, but if you're not going to listen to us, we urge you to practice birth control. We don't ever want you to feel that there's anything you can't talk to us about."

► *14. I worry about my children being molested. How can I talk about this without frightening them?*

A little-known fact is that as many as 80 percent of all child molestation cases involve someone the child knows, such as a father, a stepparent or a baby-sitter. About 90 percent of all cases involve a heterosexual male molesting a younger child. As part of a family's general discussions about sexuality, children should be taught not to go off with strangers and not to allow anyone to touch their genitals. This is also a good opportunity to teach children about their public and private parts, and public and private places. Children can be told that it's not right for anyone to touch their private parts, or for anyone else to ask them to touch theirs, no matter who it is. Some individuals force children to submit to sexual activities and make them promise never to tell anyone what happened. Should you suspect that your child has been abused in this way, it is essential to make him or her understand that such promises should not be kept. The fact that most people are decent and kind must be balanced with the reality that some people take advantage of children. A critical point is to discourage a child who has been molested from feeling any guilt or blame whatsoever. Such crimes are *always* and *entirely* the responsibility of the adult who committed them. (We recommend the video *Strong Kids, Safe Kids*, produced by Henry Winkler for Paramount.)

▶ *15. We've never talked about sex. I would like to approach the subject now, but my teenage son absolutely refuses. What should I do?*

This is a common situation, and it is appropriate for the parent to begin the conversation something like this: "I really made a mistake by waiting this long, and I wish we had talked when you were younger. I can understand why you might feel embarrassed to talk with me." Plan ahead for such discussions; have a book ready. Tell your son that you think he might be interested in it. Explain that some of the material might embarrass him, but that you're going to leave the book around just the same. The main thing is for him to understand that you are available to talk anytime he is ready. Another technique is to "hide" a book. Most teenagers are very adept at finding such "hidden" material. Sometimes the best approach is to talk about the subject in general. For example, talk about a sex-related news item in today's newspaper.

Here are some of the most frequently asked questions teenagers report they are *not likely* to ask their parents:

- Am I masturbating too much?
- Do I have homosexual tendencies?
- Am I abnormal if I have thoughts about sex with people I know, even family members?

- Are my breasts too small?
- Is my penis too small?
- How can you tell if you have VD?
- Is there something wrong with me if I remain a virgin?
- How can I say no?
- How can I tell if I'm pregnant?
- How come I have all these unexplained erections?

Think back to the time when you were growing up, and remember the kinds of questions you had about sexuality. Then you'll be able to better appreciate your child's concerns. (And for our positions on several of the above questions, refer to the previous chapter.)

► 16. *What if I find my child undressed and playing doctor with a neighbor's child?*
This is a fairly common game children play. It must be considered a normal developmental episode for preschool children. The most important thing is for parents not to lose their cool. Convey the message that you understand why they want to play with each other; tell them you'd rather they wouldn't. Indicate that you consider their genitals to be private. Then ask them to get dressed and play other games. It is not appropriate to send the other child home or to make a scene of it in any way.

► 17. *What is your opinion of high-school students having sexual intercourse?*
We're opposed to teenagers having sexual intercourse. They do not have ready access to contraception. They tend to be impulsive. The double standard is still, alas, very much with us. Also, teenage pregnancy is definitely unsound from medical, moral and psychological points of view. Another reason for this position is that young people for the most part do not—because of immaturity and inexperience—use good judgment.

While we say no to sex for teenagers, no teenager has ever asked for our consent. It is unrealistic for parents to assume that their teenagers will not have sexual relationships in the absence of parental permission. Parents still can exert a *positive* influence. Without anger, you can explain the reasons for waiting. Even young adults who are working or in college could receive similar parental messages. You might acknowledge that the decision is theirs, but if they should choose to engage in sexual intercourse it is their duty, to themselves and to their partners, to act responsibly and use contraception.

▶ *18. What should be the role of public schools in sexuality education?*

Sexuality education should be part of the regular curriculum. In most schools, it is currently excluded because of extremist pressures on school boards and administrators (Chapter 5 covers this subject in depth).

▶ *19. How can I bring up my children to respect my values?*

This depends largely on your lifestyle and the kinds of values you exemplify. You as a parent are a model for your children (which, of course, does not imply perfection), and as such you have the best opportunity of anyone they know to foster a true respect for individual differences.

Askable parents feel positive about themselves and communicate well with each other. They also have a sense of humor and recognize that not every untoward event is a trauma. Their children tend to confide in them, recognizing that their parents have a lot of common sense. Askable parents can admit, "I've made a mistake, I don't know everything." Askable parents have a better chance of bringing up children who respect their values than do those who are not responsive to their children's sexual needs and curiosity.

CHAPTER FIVE

Sexuality Education*
in the Schools

Our society devotes much time and energy coping with unwanted pregnancy, sexually transmitted diseases and related problems once they have occurred, and very little helping people prevent them in the first place. As a national effort, sex education has not even been tried. The most optimistic estimates suggest that scarcely 10 percent of our nation's young people receive adequate sex education in public schools. The remaining 90 percent are exposed to isolated lectures on basic reproductive facts—the "plumbing" of human sexuality. Since only about 25 percent of parents sex-educate their children, our society persists in producing sexually ignorant, sexually vulnerable citizens.

One apparent paradox is that Gallup and other national pollsters consistently report that between 65 and 85 percent of American adults support sex education in the schools. The Harris poll released April 19, 1983, reported that 83 percent of the public favored sex education in the schools. There were few

* Due to common usage, "sexuality education" and "sex education" will be used interchangeably to mean sexuality education as previously defined.

differences of opinion on this subject between the generations and between geographic locations.

But do we have proof that sexuality education works? In one sense, this is an unfair question because there are so few places that have effective programs. In fact, we are not familiar with a single public-school system in the entire United States that has a substantive K-12 sex education curriculum.

Early research has detailed the benefits of good sex education programs in such places as St. Paul, Minnesota, and Falls Church, Virginia. But when we get right down to it, it is extremely difficult to isolate the effects of such programs (just as it would be difficult to conduct research on how civics classes improve citizenship) in the face of such influences as peer group pressure and the mass media. In any case, the best research now available comes from the work of Professors Zelnik and Kim of Johns Hopkins University. They conclude that young women who have had sex education appear less likely to become pregnant if they are sexually active. Their studies are flawed by the fact that they didn't obtain data on the quality of the sex education received. However, their evidence does suggest that there is not a significant association between taking a course in sex education and being sexually active. In other words, their studies revealed that while sex education does not reduce sexual activity, it does not increase it, either (as some critics maintain).

We favor sex education for its intrinsic value. Simply, knowledge is worthwhile. Our clinical observations over the past thirty years suggest something else of great interest. When we try to identify the differences between those high-school students who are sexually active (engaging in sexual intercourse) and those who are virgins, some dramatic findings characteristically emerge. The virgins (both male and female) are almost all college bound, as compared to a minority of those who are sexually active. The virgins are generally more likely to take leadership roles, have a more active social life, talk more freely with their parents, are in better physical shape and are better able to control rash impulses than are nonvirgins. The virgins are better at postponing immediate gratification in exchange for later success. We can't prove it, but we're willing to wager that

most conservatively minded parents have made similar observations.

It is no accident that sex education in the schools is supported
by virtually all relevant national professional and parent groups,
including:

- American Academy of Pediatrics
- American Association of School Administrators
- American Federation of Teachers
- American Home Economics Association
- American Library Association
- American Medical Association
- American Psychiatric Association
- American Public Health Association
- American School Health Association
- Girls Clubs of America
- National Association of State Boards of Education
- National Education Association
- National School Boards Association
- National Urban League
- Young Women's Christian Association

SIECUS (the Sex Information and Education Council of the
United States), a conservative group much vilified by staunch
opponents of sex education, has taken the following position
on sex education in the schools:

> . . . programs conducted by specially trained educators
> add an important dimension to the sexuality education given
> children by their families and religious and community
> groups. Such programs must be carefully formulated by each
> community in order to respect the diversity of values and be-
> liefs represented in a public school classroom . . . with cur-
> ricula and resources appropriate to the ages of the students.

Yet we are faced with the Great American Hang-up, a secret
belief that *knowledge is harmful*—"If you tell kids about sex,
they'll do it!" (Of course, they are doing it, but without the
benefit of knowledge.)

Other questions logically arise: What should be taught? How
and by whom should it be taught? Whose values should be

conveyed? Sexuality programs cannot be taught without values. While teaching contraception, for example, the instructor must convey some basic values: (a) it is better for psychological and physiological reasons that teenagers not get pregnant, and (b) it is wrong to exploit or hurt other human beings. All other subjects, such as history, social studies, economics, are taught within the context of value systems. Why should sexuality be an exception?

There is, in teaching, a vast difference between being moral and being moralistic. Moralistic presentations seek to impose a personal point of view in a dogmatic way. It is acceptable to state, for example, that virtually all established religious groups believe it is better to wait until marriage to have sexual intercourse, but it would be moralistic to suggest that if you do engage in sex before marriage you'll go to hell. Programs are best taught with a moral perspective that encourages democratic ideals while preserving individual liberty. (See Chapter 13.)

A social-studies teacher does not say, "There are four main political systems in the world: Communism, fascism, anarchy and democracy. They are all equally good. Choose one." No, the teacher says that democracy is the best. We don't say that there are two kinds of citizens, those who vote and those who don't, and that they are equally concerned people. No, we say that the ones who don't vote are not good citizens.

Moral education encourages people to strive toward the accepted ideals of a society and presents facts which facilitate responsible decision-making. This is an important part of any sexuality education curriculum.

Even the most controversial topics may be discussed in school. Subjects such as masturbation, homosexuality and abortion could be studied in terms of the range of opinions and research that exists. Ways to prevent STD and teenage pregnancy need to be presented. Since there is no denying that people make mistakes, there would be alternatives presented to teenagers who face these problems. Who, for example, would dispute the need for good prepartum care or for the immediate treatment of oneself and one's partner once a diagnosis of STD is made?

In terms of actual curriculum guidelines, the Virginia Department of Health and Education in 1978 developed the following goals of family-life education. It should help the student to:

- develop appreciation of the roles played by family members and recognize the ways in which these roles change and interact with one another;
- understand the interpersonal attitudes, skills and responsibilities that strengthen effective family life;
- develop interpersonal skills for effective family life;
- develop a positive self-concept;
- grow in understanding of self and others;
- understand his/her physical and emotional growth and development;
- understand how reproduction occurs and life begins—plant, animal, human;
- understand that heredity and environment influence growth and development;
- understand and develop a wholesome attitude toward human sexuality as a basic factor throughout life;
- build and develop insights and values regarding human sexuality; and
- prepare a suitable foundation for responsible adulthood.

Clearly, sex education is a responsibility that optimally should be shared by parents, churches, schools and various government agencies: Toward this end, there are a number of important points to keep in mind, and a number of advocacy roles that would further the cause of producing educated, sexually responsible adults.

Parents can help themselves and their children by enrolling in or organizing adult sex education courses and seminars. They can seek direction from a variety of sources already established in most communities, such as church groups and PTAs. On hundreds of college campuses, at health centers and social agencies, there are sex education workshops organized specifically for teachers, parents and expectant parents.

It is of the greatest importance that parents support well-planned sex education programs in their children's schools.

Parents can attend school board meetings and voice their support for the programs as well as contribute their ideas on how they should be structured. Write letters to superintendents and principals asking them to incorporate sexuality education curricula into the schools. If a controversy develops over the programs in the local media, don't be afraid to compose a letter to the editor. It is well known that educators are loath to plan and implement sex education when they are unaware of the sentiments of the community; they need and appreciate such input from parents. Those who are willing to support such programs are urged to obtain a copy of Irving Dickman's monograph entitled "Winning the Battle for Sex Education," available from SIECUS.

As for teachers, an unflappable demeanor, a strong credibility, a sense of humor and a compassionate nature are characteristics which are paramount. This is true for all teachers, but especially for those involved in sex education programs. Teachers should be able to establish a genuine rapport with their students and be prepared to help, should a student approach them with a personal problem. Assistance could include referring students to public or private agencies where, for instance, they can obtain confidential tests for pregnancy and STD, plus follow-up treatment if needed. Some students are reluctant to discuss personal problems or feelings with a school nurse or with their parents, yet many have been known to confide in a teacher they trust.

The sensitivity of the subject and the inexperience of school administrators in dealing with a few vocal opponents has contributed to the failure of sex education in the public schools. Nevertheless, many school courses could be enhanced greatly by incorporating information about human sexuality into them. Subjects such as psychology, home economics, English, social studies and biology lend themselves logically to the inclusion of sex education. Home economics is especially adaptable in this regard, because it is the type of course where the principles of parenting are taught. (Don't assume that this instruction is for girls only; home economics should be mandatory for both sexes.) And there's no reason why topics such as the changing size of the American family and shifting attitudes toward human reproduction cannot be dovetailed into American- and world-history courses.

Our view is that a quality sex education program—perhaps more appropriately entitled "family-life education"—must include the following principles:

1. *Enhancing the self-concept*—cultivating the self: that is a prerequisite for establishing mature relationships and acting sexually responsible.
2. *Preparing for marriage and parenthood*—understanding the interpersonal skills and responsibilities that strengthen family life.
3. *Understanding love* as the basic component of a person's sexuality, including help in deciding "how you can tell if you are really in love."
4. *Preparing for making responsible decisions* in critical areas of sexuality, based on a universal value of not hurting or using others.
5. *Helping people understand the need for equal opportunities* for males and females. Schools have a responsibility to discourage sexism.
6. *Helping people develop tolerance and appreciation* for people who don't conform to the traditional norms regarding marriage and childbearing.
7. *Contributing to knowledge and understanding of the sexual dimension of our lives*—including the realization that we are sexual beings even *before* birth and have sexual needs and a sexual identity throughout life. It includes an appreciation for the wide range of sexuality; that sexual expression is not limited to heterosexual, genital intercourse; and that sexual expression goes beyond reproduction.

In family-life education, feelings, communication and values should be the focus.

The most successful programs will be those which raise young people's level of self-esteem and teach them the facts of physiology and contraception they need to know. Girls especially must be helped to cope with the double standard, which implies that while boys may experiment sexually, girls may not, or that girls must bear the full responsibility for any offspring resulting from out-of-wedlock births. Young people also need guidance on subtler issues, such as how to respond to the lines that boys in every society use to persuade girls to have sexual relations with them. Girls can be told that sex is never a test of love, and boys told that using another human being to satisfy selfish desires is wrong.

Young people who feel good about themselves, and who feel comfortable with their values in the midst of their own culture, are more likely to receive information openly and use it to their own best advantages. In this atmosphere, the transmission of values and information through sex education programs is most likely to be successful.

We must make it clear what the extremist opposition is all about. Sexuality education used to be equated with Communism, but that's not very popular anymore. Now the attacks focus on humanism. The American Humanist Association includes both religious and nonreligious adherents and has a legitimate moral point of view which we support. However, there are those like Dr. Tim LeHaye who claim that *secular humanism* dominates and controls our public-school system. We publicly offered a $10,000 reward if he or anyone could certify that a single public-school system in the entire United States has a secular-humanist curriculum. Dr. LeHaye made inquiries about the reward but has not claimed it. The secular humanists are, in fact, a small group of a few thousand intellectuals who are known as highly ethical people and who believe that religion detracts from society's efforts to improve conditions in the world (a position we do not endorse). Despite their small numbers and minimal influence, secular humanists have been erroneously identified as the major corrupters of today's youth.

Censorship represents another form of opposition to sex education and is a major problem now in many parts of the country. The American Library Association's Office of Intellectual Freedom reports that the number of complaints concerning the removal of books from school and public libraries has increased *tenfold* during the past decade. The Gablers of Longview, Texas, want to ban from our public schools textbooks which do not agree with their highly moralistic, idiosyncratic view of what sexuality or patriotism is all about. They are, unfortunately, quite successful in their campaign. Their main view: "Too many textbooks leave students to make up their own minds about things."

Another attack is to cite Scandinavia as a center of moral decay. In fact the Scandinavian countries have higher standards of living than we do and have almost eliminated poverty. Only in the last decade have they had compulsory sex education, and the evidence is clear that there has been a significant decline in unintended pregnancy, venereal disease and sex crimes there in the last several years. We thoroughly researched this issue ourselves while in Sweden and Denmark in the summer of 1982. One enormous difference emerged: More than 80 percent of Scandinavian teenagers use birth control the first time they have sexual intercourse, in contrast to 20 percent in the United States.

It would be instructive to quote from *Guidelines for Sex Education in the Swedish School System* developed in 1974 and still in effect. The following are selections from these guidelines which teachers in "decadent" Sweden are encouraged to teach:

> The Commission has found that the fundamental values indicate that the following ethical guidelines, among others, should be maintained and promoted in the course of teaching:
>
> —A worth-while aim is to combine sexual life, togetherness, and respect for the integrity of the other person. *This, in the Commission's opinion, is a central value judgment that should set the tone of sex education as a whole.*
>
> —There apply to sexual relationships the same demands for consideration to others and responsibility for the consequences of action as hold in other fields of life. This means, first and foremost, that no fellow being should be regarded exclusively as a means for the satisfaction of another's interests and needs. In the sexual as in other fields, any form of mental pressure or physical violence constitutes a violation of the other person's integrity.
>
> —Teaching should support a standard that is embraced by the great majority of the Swedish population, namely the rejection of "unfaithfulness." By unfaithfulness should be

meant in this context a disloyalty rather than a sexual act in itself.

—Teaching should reject the traditional double morality by which moral sentence is passed upon women for actions that a man can commit with impunity. The rejection of sexual double morality is one aspect of the function of teaching to combat prejudice regarding sexual roles.

—The demand for equal rights entails also that teaching should argue against racial discrimination in the sexual field. As immigration continues, this question can become increasingly topical.

—The condemnation of variations in the direction of people's sexual urge should be counteracted, and a considerate attitude to such phenomena promoted.

—Teaching should promote recognition of the right to a sexual life on the part of the physically and mentally handicapped, the mentally diseased, the inmates of prisons, and others tied to institutions. Prejudice against the sexual life of the elderly should be combatted.

—Teaching should proclaim sexual tolerance in the sense of respecting the rights of others to speak for, and live by, sexual standards that oneself rejects. Such tolerance, however, cannot apply to attitudes in the sexual field which are incompatible with the fundamental values which have to be promoted. Teaching, for instance, cannot take a tolerant view of racial discrimination in this field, or of double morality.

Proposals thus far have examined the fundamental values which teaching should maintain and promote. Among the *controversial values* the Commission lists the following, which should thus be treated without taking sides.

—Ethical attitudes to abortion. On this question, some groups consider that abortion should only occur on specific medical and other grounds, while others consider that the wishes of the woman should be paramount. The school cannot be involved in arguments in favor of either point of view. It is of the greatest importance, however, that the arguments of both groups be correctly reported.

—Premarital sexual relationships with the person one intends to marry or permanently live with are regarded as self-evidently acceptable by the great majority of the Swedish population. About half of those with a personal Christian faith, however, are convinced that sexual life together in accordance with God's will can take place only within marriage. Such parents and their children must be able to assume that their view will be presented in the schools in a proper and respectful manner. Teaching must not take sides against their view. It is another matter that teaching must devote considerable time to the questions of personal premarital relationships.

We can learn a lot from the Swedes!

There are parents who love and want the best for their children, and who are also uncertain about sexuality education in the schools. We encourage such parents to become involved in the planning and implementation of sex education programs, so that they can see for themselves what is going on. In fact, school-based programs need the commitment of more concerned parents who share a vital interest in their children's welfare. We believe that once parents who oppose sexuality education better understand the programs, they will choose to support them.

The bulk of the opposition to sex education, however, comes from small, articulate, well-organized extremist and sometimes fanatical groups. If they represent 5 percent of the population, we would be astonished. Nevertheless, superintendents and principals of schools are invariably overly responsive to these groups. They want to avoid controversy. Some administrators and school boards have lost sight of the fact that wrestling with controversial issues is at the very heart of the democratic process.

Interestingly enough, school systems which do have programs—such as that in the state of Maryland, which has had a good Family Life and Human Development curriculum for the past ten years—are fully supported by students and parents. Parents have an option not to permit their children to take these sex education courses. Over the years thousands of students have been sex-educated, with less than 2 percent of the parents opting to remove their children from these classes. Where is all this massive opposition to sex education that groups including the John Birch Society, Motorede, Moral Majority, POSSE, MOMS, Citizens for Excellence in Education, POPE, CUF and the Christian's Crusade are trying to persuade the American public exists?

The "antis" are not above outrageous lies. For a while they circulated the spurious story that a female teacher undressed in front of her sex education class in order to make the course relevant. A "book burning" team in West Virginia stated that our book *Facts About Sex for Today's Youth* had explicit drawings of sexual positions. We looked again and couldn't find any. Another critic described our work as the "glorification of immodesty, impurity and sexual permissiveness" and went on to say that our views can be expressed as follows: "Any form of sexual expression is 'healthy' and 'moral' if pleasurable, hygienic and voluntary."

Of course, this critic left out words that we do use such as "adult," "mature," "nonexploitative," "guilt-free," "enhancing of the person," "consenting." The most frequent accusation leveled at sex educators is that they preach to teenagers, "If it feels good, do it." This is an absurd fabrication, and we know of no sex educator who endorses that position for young people or adults, for that matter.

Another leading opponent of sex education described our publications in the following manner:

> I believe they're right. It's educational. But what are they educating them for? If gals want to grow up to run a house of prostitution, they know exactly what supplies are needed. I think it's a demoralizing promotion by Communism. If they get the young people interested in sex, they can demoralize the country and just walk in and take it over. That's the Communist procedure.

If you are not convinced that the antisex educators are well-organized and serious, read this quote from a strategy pamphlet that has been widely circulated among them:

> [Go] to school board meetings in your town and other towns— applaud and groan at the right times, and if necessary, stomp your feet and scream. The more brazen you are, the more attention you'll get. Don't refer to school programs as family life and sex education but simply call them sex programs. It'll upset them, and when they're upset they don't think as well.

Parents and society in general would be wise to keep in mind the admonition of the eighteenth-century Jewish sage Baal Shem-Tov, who said, "The world is full of people who in the guise of piety are ready to harass others."

More sober opponents like to cite statistics which "prove" that sex education programs in the United States and elsewhere have failed to discourage irresponsible sexual behavior among the young. Generally they make the mistake of lumping together both optimal and inadequate programs, and then drawing sweeping conclusions based on the faulty evidence. Nevertheless, a good general principle is: *Don't overstate the value of sex education in the schools.* It can transmit information, reduce sex-related guilt, foster a sense of responsibility, and even reduce rates of unintended pregnancies and STDs by 10–20 percent over a five- to ten-year period. But without reducing the most compelling reasons for irresponsible sexual behavior, namely racism, sexism, poverty and individual vulnerability, officials should not hope for overwhelming success.

In addition, programs conducted in schools where there are big discipline problems and low morale can certainly not be expected to have good results. Such courses would simply not have any credibility in the eyes of the students.

What a pity that we still must share the view of the author of a book about sex education in Britain (*My Mother Said . . . The Way Young People Learned About Sex and Birth Control*, by Christine Farrell): that neither males nor females are "currently given as much information as they would wish for, at an age they think appropriate, or from a source which they regard as authoritative."

There is concern among some parents that sex educators are attempting to replace parents as the primary sex educators of children. There is simply no basis for this fear. Even the best, most comprehensive sex education program seeks only to supplement the primary responsibilities of parents. The schools, religions and governmental agencies all have a secondary role in providing information and services for young people; the primary responsibility for sex-educating children from birth to adulthood always has been and must remain in the home. Parents provide the love, warmth and caring that are the foundations of many future values and attitudes concerning sexuality, and family life can only be strengthened by parents who take an active role in communicating with their own children.

CHAPTER SIX

What Children Need to Know: The Preschool and Preteen Years

*I*n a questionnaire given to 450 Syracuse University undergraduates, more than 50 percent thought that their parents were comfortable with their own sexuality. But when asked, "As you were growing up, what would you wish your parents had told you about sex?," about 90 percent of these students indicated that sex was not honestly discussed in their homes.

I wish my parents had canned the stork story and fairy tale explanations—and told me the truth.

I wish my parents sat me down and told me about sex instead of just saying "don't let no one in your pants."

I wish that my parents had talked to me about sex—going beyond menstruation, pubic hair, etc.

I wish my parents had been more open about sex and not treated it as a big dark secret to be discovered and experienced after marriage.

I wish they had told me not to feel so inhibited about my body. I wish they told me that there was nothing wrong with making love with someone if it is right and special.

I wish my parents spoke to me more about birth control and let me know that in trouble I could turn to them.

I wish Mom had told me that first sexual encounters—meaning intercourse, per se—would probably be fairly disappointing in most ways!

Only about 10 percent of the students seemed to be satisfied with their parents' efforts or nonefforts at sex education.

The clearest message to emerge from our work in sexuality education is that children appreciate openness and candor at an early age. Parents who rarely communicate with their children when young have the most difficulty talking with teenagers, whom they finally perceive as being old enough to understand. Often the credibility of parents is diminished when they give the impression that any area *except* human sexuality is open for discussion.

It might be instructive to know a little about how one of us—Sol Gordon—got into this field. I was working in a child-guidance clinic at a time when sexuality was not much discussed. This was no accident, because virtually no medical school or professional school of psychology, social work or nursing included courses in sexuality at that time. Thus, doctors and other professionals who were supposed to know the most often didn't know any more than the people who were asking the questions. This amounted to a conspiracy of silence, even in the heyday of psychoanalysis when sex was assumed to be the root of all neurosis.

Under the circumstances, any discussion was so abstract that it didn't help average people understand their own sexuality, their children's sexuality or some of the conflicts between the two. Practical questions regarding such topics as penis or vagina size, the clitoris, the role of communication in sexual functioning, and a host of others went unanswered.

Once, as part of a study, we asked one hundred teenagers (fifty boys and fifty girls) if their parents had talked to them about sex. Each one said no. Then we asked the parents if they had spoken to their children about this subject. All said that they had in fact done so. These contradictory results were fascinating because one seldom gets such widely divergent findings. We pursued the matter eagerly, asking the teenagers if they really couldn't remember or perhaps weren't telling the truth. When we pushed the teenagers harder still, virtually all of the girls remembered that their mothers had talked to them about menstruation. The rest of the communication could be summed up in one word: *Don't*. The boys were less impressed by our efforts to jog their memories. However, once we spoke of the ritual of "going out for a walk," about half of the boys remembered it taking place when they were about eleven years old. We decided they remembered an awkward discussion about the birds and the bees, both father and son so embarrassed that very little real communication took place. Some did recall the father ending the conversation with the remark that if worse came to worse, the son could always find some condoms in the father's drawer.

This research is twenty years old now, but it still seems to contain elements of truth. Whenever large mixed adult audiences are told about it, there is nervous laughter suggesting that perhaps it had been part of their own experience. Their reaction reinforces our strong belief that sex should not be something one limits to a single talk, or even to an occasional talk coupled to significant physical developments in a child's life. Sexuality education should be an *ongoing process*. Becoming an askable parent starts long before the child goes to school. The parent who has discussed sexuality openly with the young child can expect the teenager to share confidences later.

Parents need to understand what experiences affect children in their early years, especially if they are to help them develop positive attitudes toward themselves and others. In this light, we'd like to share with readers a letter we received from a mother who feared that she and her husband were not very successful in their efforts to help and guide their children. The letter highlights a dilemma which is faced by all parents, and which demands that we be realistic in our appraisal of parent–child relationships.

It may sound strange to other people when we say this, but my husband and I know that we have been good parents. We've raised our children firmly but lovingly, have made sure they know what our values are, and have given them a good sex education. Thus, it disturbs me tremendously when our children behave in ways which contradict so strongly what we've taught them. For instance, our 10-year-old son insists on calling some of his friends "faggot," even though we've told him many times that this is offensive. My husband and I wind up looking at each other and saying, "He didn't get it from us"—but where do these things come from?

Our answer:

Your question illustrates so well how outside influences sometimes overwhelm even our best intentions. We can guide our children, but we can't exercise full control over them. A good approach is to make sure that children know the meaning of the derogatory words they're using. Then focus on your own attitude rather than criticizing them. For example, get across the message that you would appreciate it if they wouldn't use such terms, and you would feel much better if they were a bit more sensitive on this subject. Ask the children to think through how they would feel if their friend or sibling really was a homosexual.

Such incidents should not be the occasion for parental self-doubt or feelings of failure. The effects of talking openly about sexuality and other important topics may not be immediately apparent, but these things have a way of taking hold, provided that we're not too impatient. As Lisa Strick summarized her January 1983 article in *Woman's Day*: "Talking about sex at home—openly and truthfully—won't guarantee that your children will be virgins when they marry. But it might prevent them from becoming parents before they've had a chance to find out what it is to be grown up."

WHAT YOU NEED TO KNOW
ABOUT INFANTILE SEXUALITY

Sexual pleasure is not confined to stimulation of the genitals, nor is all pleasant physical contact related to sex. This is true even of the youngest of babies, who learn about the pleasures of physical contact through constant loving fondling. Parents stroke, kiss and cuddle their babies, and the babies respond with affection. They find great satisfaction in using their mouths when eating and when sucking on their toes or other objects.

An infant is learning even though he or she does not yet talk. The infant will use this early learning later in life. What infants learn about love, affection and physical contact will affect their sexual attitudes and behaviors when they become biologically ready to have children, in the period called puberty. Many of a person's sexual feelings and attitudes are determined before the age of five.

For instance, toilet-training before children are ready can create feelings of self-doubt, guilt and shame. These feelings may trouble the youngsters for the rest of their lives, though they probably won't even be aware of them. Suppose that a child has an "accident" and is punished, or simply is told that he or she is "bad" or "dirty." If the child is not capable or old enough to control elimination, he or she may become (honestly) confused and develop serious feelings of anxiety, guilt and inferiority.

Children need to be handled with patience and understanding. This means that parents must stop and think before punishing too quickly, deciding as honestly as possible whether they are doing so for the child's good or merely for their own convenience, even as a reaction to their own, possibly unjustified fears.

This applies as well to infants beginning to discover and explore their bodies. If parents slap a child's fingers or pull the hand away for playing with the genitals even though they coo and smile and comment on how cute the child looks when playing with his or her toes, the child will be confused and may associate the genitals with feelings of guilt and shame.

No one expects babies who are barely old enough to walk, talk or know where the bathroom is to be anything but innocent and carefree. Only when children are old enough to go to the bathroom on their own can parents teach them not to touch their sex organs in public, in the same way they are taught not to suck their thumbs.

We have already discussed such issues as masturbation, nudity in the home and obscenities (see Chapter 4, "Becoming an Askable Parent"). Treating the child's developing growth and awareness in these areas with respect and acceptance is perhaps more important in the early years of life than at any other time.

Sometimes we forget the fact that sexuality is something we are rather than something we do. When a baby is born, our first question often is, "What is it? Is it a boy or a girl?" We then program the child according to its sex as he or she gets older. It may be less popular these days for children to be identified in terms of dress—blue for boys and pink for girls—but stereotyping remains a fact of life for many youngsters. We see it in terms of behavior identified as appropriate only for girls or for boys, in families where remarks like "That's not for a boy" are common. Boys and girls get the impression that nothing is more terrible than "acting" like a member of the opposite sex.

The following letter from a mother demonstrates how volatile an issue this can become in some homes, truly a stage-center conflict which nobody is likely to "win" unless it is handled with an appreciation for the child's dynamics.

> My husband and I have strong differences of opinion about our four-year-old son who occasionally likes to play house with his girlfriends. He seems to be a big disappointment to my husband because of his apparent lack of interest in so-called "male" activities such as playing with trucks and guns. I'm sure that in the back of my husband's mind is the idea that if we don't discourage our son's "effeminate" activities now, he'll become a homosexual later on.

Our answer:

> It is always difficult when parents disagree. You might want to tell your husband that the more he criticizes your son's behavior, the more unhappy your son will become, not the more masculine. The very best approach would be for him to make it a point to spend time with the child alone, slowly and gradually involving him in activities that your husband finds more appropriate. There is no real substitute for working on an improved relationship between father and son first, before focusing on the specific "problems" of your son.

Parents do worry about sexual confusion and sexual identity. Even "liberal" parents can become concerned when their little boys appear to enjoy dressing up in women's clothing. There is somewhat less concern for girls who take on "tomboyish" traits. Most often, but not necessarily, such behavior is a transitional stage and nothing more. Our advice is to test it out and see if not "fussing" makes other interests become predominant. Should these cross-sexual traits maintain themselves over a long period of time, they may indicate gender confusion. Yet one should be concerned only if they seem to reflect a basic neurotic trend in the development of the child, a trend symptomatic of other areas of maladjustment. A child who makes friends, enjoys life and is relatively free of symptoms—of stuttering, failure to thrive, bedwetting beyond the fourth or fifth year, or extreme introversion—and who, at the same time, takes on the so-called sensitivity of the opposite sex (even in terms of the popular stereotypes), may be evidencing a background for creativity and good emotional development. Our advice is to be concerned only if the behavior seems to reflect a general disorganization of the personality.

Why do parents need to think about these situations or questions before they arise? Such thought provides a certain rehearsal behavior. Even the most sophisticated and alert parents can get confused when confronted by their children at unexpected moments with such questions as "Where did I come from?" and "How did I get into you?" Parents should think beforehand of their responses. Farther on in this chapter we list a number of questions typical of preschool children, along with our suggested responses.

You may feel that a child's question is inappropriate at that moment, as, from your adult perspective, it may be. But the very fact that the child asked it indicates its appropriateness from his or her perspective. A child should never be given the impression that he or she has asked the wrong question, that the timing is wrong, or that there is something wrong with the child for asking the question in the first place. Parents may prefer that everything be done according to their expectations, in line with certain developmental stages or at points when they personally feel ready, but children are full of surprises. That's part of the excitement of raising children.

SOME PARENTAL CONCERNS

There are specific sexually related questions or situations about which parents may be concerned. For example, how should you react to a child who wants to climb into bed with you? We feel that this is okay. Many adults recall that some of their most pleasant experiences took place early in childhood when they could have a lot of fun with their parents in bed. Some parents worry about sexual stimulation, but most are quite comfortable with the idea. Even if they find themselves becoming stimulated by this contact, they are able to acknowledge the sensual delight of loving their children so closely. There is a natural warmth between parents and children, and sharing this physical affection provides children with a sound basis for their later capacity to love and eventually be loving parents themselves. In any case, it usually becomes a playful, "roughhouse" experience, rather than one that is specifically erotic.

On the other hand, we don't think it is good policy to allow children to sleep with parents. If your child has traumatic dreams or nightmares and wants the comfort of sleeping with you, it might be a good idea to say, "I'll stay with you for a while until you fall asleep." Or to invite the child to come to your bed for a while until comforted, then carry the youngster back to bed.

It is quite common for children to have upsetting nightmares, and one shouldn't dismiss the experience by simply telling them not to worry about it. Parents can tell children that they know nightmares are frightening and that everyone has them at one time or another. The important thing is to reassure them that all they have to do is open their eyes and the nightmare will disappear.

We share parental concerns about television, not because of the exposure to sexual information, but because of the violence. It is wise for parents to exert some control over television-watching habits, especially if indulged as a substitute for activity, learning and achieving.

The early school age is the time for developing basic academic skills and establishing good study habits. The old notion that this constitutes a "latency" period when children are not particularly interested in anything sexual is a myth perpetuated by Freudian diehards. We've rarely met children of school age who were not aware and excited, interested in and affected by the sexual aspects of their lives. They'll ask questions and be curious.

They'll certainly observe what's happening on television. They'll notice pregnancies, and they'll wonder where the puppies next door came from. This is a good age to respond candidly and freely to all pertinent sexually oriented questions. (By "pertinent" we mean to exclude questions about your own private sexual life.)

SEXUAL ABUSE OF CHILDREN

We feel that this chapter presents the best opportunity for us to address a painful, difficult issue: sexual molestation of children. Sexual abuse may occur to children of any age, from infants through the teenage years. (The most common age is from eleven to fourteen years old.) A realistic understanding of molestation is essential for parents, particularly since this area has been clouded by misinformation and taboos.

The National Center on Child Abuse and Neglect has estimated that of the one million child-abuse cases reported each year, 12 percent were victims of sexual molestation. Most were girls abused by fathers, stepfathers and close relatives. Louise Armstrong, in her powerful book *Kiss Daddy Goodnight*, has suggested that sexual molestation of children is so common it would seem not to be a taboo at all; talking about it is.

Child molestation crosses all social, economic and racial boundaries and affects a wide range of family situations. Stereotypes which portray the offenders as obviously neurotic, lecherous, "dirty old men," even psychotic, are inaccurate. The phenomenon does usually seem to be accompanied by manifestations of low self-esteem and of self-destructive behavior. Incest can continue only in secret, and the families involved are typically isolated from friends and the mainstream of life.

We strongly recommend that parents of young children read to them our book entitled *A Better Safe than Sorry Book: A Family Guide for Sexual Assault Prevention.*

The Federal Child Abuse Prevention and Treatment Act of 1974 defined child abuse, including sexual abuse or exploitation, as injury or maltreatment of a child "by a person who is responsible for the child's welfare." The National Center of Child Abuse and Neglect has adopted a broader definition:

> . . . contacts or interactions between a child and an adult when the child is being used for the sexual stimulation of the perpetrator or another person. Sexual abuse may also be committed by a person under the age of 18 when that person is either significantly older than the victim or when the perpetrator is in a position of power or control over another child.

The very nature of the power relationship between parents or other adults and children often inhibits the youngsters from revealing the act of sexual advances made against them. Subtle or overt threats are often made to discourage exposing the situation, or the child is sufficiently sophisticated to perceive some of the consequences: loss of family income, police or social-service intervention and subsequent court trials, the possibility of psychiatric treatment or incarceration, the breakup of the family and public shame. Once in the open, the situation must be handled sensitively for the child's sake; interviews, medical examinations and court procedures must be conducted with an awareness of the child's acute fears and anxieties.

Not long ago a close friend of ours from the Midwest called one evening in a near-hysterical state; her twelve-year-old daughter had been approached sexually by her grandfather, the woman's father. The grandfather, as is often the case, was a responsible member of the community, a proverbial "pillar" of family rectitude. The child's experience had triggered a memory the mother had long repressed: when she was the same age as her daughter, the same man had sexually molested her. As a young teenager, she had dealt with it fairly well, told no one, and repressed the incident altogether. Though she had managed reasonably well to overcome her feelings of fear and guilt, in retrospect she realized that it had inhibited her sexual responsiveness and healthy adjustment to adulthood. When she confronted her father with the truth, he denied it absolutely and acted as if she had imagined the whole thing. Her own mother accused her of hating her father and plotting to destroy the family.

These reactions are not atypical; only a fraction of child-molestation incidents are brought to the attention of authorities, and even fewer are successfully prosecuted. In truth, no absolute guidelines can be set for the disposition of such cases. Not all should be dealt with outside the context of the family, nor come under legal jurisdiction. We are, however, convinced that being molested is often a traumatizing experience for the child involved even though most recover with strong support.

Once upon a time, a parent's precaution was simply to tell a child never to accept candy or rides from a stranger. But strangers, as modern statistics point out, represent only about 25 percent of the offenders (to be sure, when it does involve a stranger, enticements are usually involved). Parents as well as caretakers need to convey a somewhat different message to children. They should tell them that no one—stranger, neighbor, relative or family member—has the right to touch or fondle their genitals. The child should understand that even if it is someone he or she knows and loves, it is still not right.

Generally speaking, the message to the child might be: "If someone ever touches you there or asks or forces you to touch them, please tell us right away. Say no to the person and get away from him if you can. Even if the person makes you promise not to tell anyone, that is a promise you should not keep. If you are threatened or forced to do things, you may have to go along with them, but even if you 'swear to God' not to tell your mother, God doesn't expect you to keep promises that hurt you. Whenever someone says, 'Don't tell your mother,' that's a good way of knowing that whatever they are asking you to do is wrong." Children can be told these things without being caused excessive alarm or scared unduly.

Relatives as well as the victims themselves often develop a keen desire for revenge and punishment for the molester. But jail and retribution are rarely as rehabilitative as counseling and therapy can be. Child-abuse hotlines and special counseling centers now exist in every state. They offer support, counseling, referrals and legal assistance to victims as well as victimizers. With over eight hundred chapters nationwide, Parents Anonymous (PA) is a major resource (toll free, 800-421-0353; in California, 800-352-0386; or, if there is a local chapter, call it).

Recently, some researchers have suggested that the pain and trauma associated with incidents of child molestation have been exaggerated. Yet few if any victims have come forward to declare that they benefited from the experiences. The absence of trauma is hardly evidence of a positive effect; many victims survive the experience without suffering terribly, but others live afterward with enormous feelings of guilt, anger and outrage.

If a child informs a parent that he or she has been sexually molested, there are things which the parent can do to help alleviate the child's suffering. First (and this will be difficult), try to control your own anxiety level. If the child senses that you are devastated by the situation, it could magnify the child's own misery. Parents should never say things like "Why did you let him do it?" or "Why didn't you run away?" Such questions imply that the incident was somehow the child's fault. We want to state unequivocally that it is *always* the responsibility of the molester. No matter how "seductive" or "flirtatious" a little girl might seem, she is not to be blamed for an adult male's inability to control his impulses.

Perhaps most importantly, comfort the child. Let her know that you still love and value her. The child may appear fearful for a time afterward and may need immense reassurance of her continuing worth, safety and acceptance in the family. In a very important sense, how the child ultimately responds to the event, and how well or badly her self-esteem fares, depends on how the situation is responded to in the family. (The best book for parents on the subject, a book we highly recommend, is *The Silent Children: A Parent's Guide to the Prevention of Child Sexual Abuse*, by Lynn Sanford.)

PRETEENS

There are two areas where parents must accept responsibility: preparing girls for the onset of menstruation, and preparing boys for nocturnal emissions. The child should know well in advance, so that the events do not come as traumatic surprises. And girls should be told about nocturnal emissions, just as boys should be told about menstruation. In fact, girls and boys should be informed fully of these and other developments affecting the opposite sex as well as their own.

When a girl is no older than ten, a mother or female relative should specifically demonstrate the proper method of using sanitary napkins. The demonstration should be accompanied by a very positive explanation of menstruation as a normal and healthy bodily process that all girls first experience between the ages of eleven and fifteen or so. It is vital that the young girl look upon her growth into womanhood as a positive step in her development.

Also around the age of ten, boys should be told by either the mother or the father that wet dreams happen to almost all boys and are a normal stage of male development, usually first experienced between the ages of eleven and fifteen or so. The boy should be told that you understand his bedclothes and linens may get wet, and that he can put them privately into the hamper. It should be made clear that wet dreams are related to sexual impulses and thoughts and will occur less frequently as he gets older. By the time he has opportunities for regular sexual outlets, they are likely to cease altogether.

IN THEIR OWN WORDS
Children under six often ask very good questions. Here are some of them, along with some suggested responses.

► *Where did I come from?*
You began in a special place inside Mommy called the uterus. When you were ready to be born you came out through Mommy's vagina. Both Mommy and Daddy were needed to get you started.

► *How did I get inside you?*
When Daddy and I felt very cuddly in bed, Daddy put his penis into my vagina. A tiny seed called a sperm from Daddy met a tiny egg called an ovum inside me. That's how you got started. You were so small that I wasn't sure at first if a baby was beginning to grow inside me. You grew and grew in my uterus for a long time. Then you were born.

► *Where was I before I got inside you?*
You weren't anywhere. Daddy and I got you started. When I felt you growing inside we were very happy.

► *How long did I have to grow until you saw me?*

It took nine months for you to grow in my uterus before you were born. But I knew that you were there. You began kicking when you had been in my uterus only around five months. You didn't kick hard, just enough to let me know that you were there and to say, "Hi." Plus I grew very big in front.

► *Why does Jim have a penis and I don't?*

That's one of the differences between boys and girls. Girls have a vagina and boys don't. Only girls have a vulva. Do you know what part of you is called the vulva? Do you know where your vagina is?

► *A three-year-old boy taking a shower with his dad wants to know, "Why is your penis bigger than mine?"*

As you get older your penis will become larger and be like mine.

► *A four-year-old girl taking a shower with her mother points to the mother's breasts and asks, "How come you have two and I don't have any?"*

As you grow older you will develop breasts, too.

► *How do babies get food before they are born?*

Every time the mother eats something, the baby gets a little of that food. Also, every time the mother breathes, the baby receive a little oxygen.

► *Did you know that I would be a girl before I was born?*

No, mothers and fathers do not usually know that. All they know is that they are going to have a baby. When the baby is born, if it has a vagina, it's a girl. If it has a penis, it's a boy.

► *Five-year-old Eddie is having a bath with his four-year-old sister, Suzy. She notices that Eddie's penis is hard and sticking straight out. She asks her mother why.*

Eddie has what is called an erection. This happens to all boys occasionally. It's a nice feeling when it happens.

► *Does it hurt to have a baby?*

Yes, having a baby does hurt. Do you remember when you fell and bumped your head? It hurt for just a little while and then you forgot about it. It's the same thing when you have a baby. It usually hurts only a little while.

► *Why can't I sleep with you?*

Because Daddy and I sleep in the same bed. We like privacy at night.

► *What's privacy?*

Privacy means that you want to be alone sometimes. Occasionally, two people like Mommy and Daddy enjoy being together without anyone else there. You too want to be by yourself at times. Then you can sing and play and no one will disturb you.

► *Aunt Jackie doesn't feed Baby Alice from her breast. How come?*

Because Aunt Jackie decided that she would rather feed Baby Alice from a bottle. Every mother makes her own decision about that.

► *Mom, will you tell Emily where babies come from? Her mom won't tell her. Her mom said those things were dirty and she shouldn't ask questions.*

That's too bad. You and I know that isn't so. I don't think that there are any dirty questions. I want you to ask me anything you want to know. I'll try to answer. I hope that Emily's mom in time will talk to her in the same way you and I are talking now.

► *Whom do you love most, Daddy or me?*

I love each of you differently. I love Grandma and Grandpa differently also. There are many kinds of love.

► *Can I love myself?*

When you look into the mirror and smile at yourself, or when you feel good about you, then you love yourself. It's very important that you love yourself, because then you can love other people and they will love you.

IN THEIR OWN WORDS

Children who are six, seven, eight or almost nine might have questions like these:

► *Does every woman have a baby?*

No, not every woman has a baby. Women who have sexual intercourse with men can have babies. When a seed called a sperm from a man comes together with an egg called an ovum from a woman, a baby gets started.

Not every woman wants to have a baby. Most who do want children have only one or two. So, if we don't want to have a baby we use birth control when we have sexual intercourse.

► *What is birth control?*

Mommy and Daddy have sex because we enjoy it. It's one of the nice things grown-ups do. When we are not trying to have a baby, we use a special pill [device, method] that keeps Mommy from getting pregnant. Pregnant means that a woman is going to have a baby.

► *How old is grown up?*

A lot of people think that grown up is when you are over eighteen years old or when you get married.

► *Can I have a baby now and can Jimmy be its daddy?*

You can start having babies only after you start to menstruate. But you should not have a baby until you can take care of it. Jimmy is also not ready. It's better to wait until you are grown up and married.

► *What's a tampon for?*

A tampon is used by girls and women when they are menstruating in order to protect their clothing.

► *Do I have to be married to have children?*

It would be better for the baby if you and the baby's father were married. It's very hard to bring up children by yourself. It can be done—some people do it. When you are older, you'll want to decide many things about your future. One of those things will be which job you want. Another will be where you want to live, and still another will be if you want to get married and have children. You will have lots of time to think about those things.

► *How does a baby get out of a mommy's tummy?*

First of all, the baby is not in Mommy's tummy. I know it

looks that way to you. A baby rests in a special place called the uterus. When it is ready to be born it comes out through the vagina. The vagina doesn't seem big enough, but it stretches so the baby can come out.

Most babies are born in this way, but not all. When a mother is having trouble giving birth to a baby, doctors sometimes perform an operation called a Caesarean section. This is a simple surgical technique. Doctors make an incision—a cut—in the mother's lower abdomen. Then they remove the baby from the uterus. It doesn't take long, and the baby isn't hurt by it. The mother heals quickly and is back on her feet within a few days. Many mothers have this done, and children born this way are just like any others.

► *How does a baby get started?*

Before a man and a woman have sexual intercourse, they lie together making love. During that time the man's penis hardens and the woman's vagina lubricates. The man puts his penis into the woman's vagina when she feels ready. After a little while sperm comes out of the man's penis. If sperm unite with an ovum from the woman's ovaries, a baby gets started.

► *What if someone wants to touch my private parts?*

(Private parts are your breasts, vulva, penis and rectum.)

Tell him—it's usually a boy or a man—that you don't want him to do it, even if it's someone you know well. It's not right. You know it isn't right because the person says, "Don't tell your mommy." This means that you should tell your mommy right away. A child should be able to tell his or her mommy or daddy anything.

► *What is a prostitute?*

A prostitute is a person who is willing to have sexual relations for money. It is not legal in our country, but it happens.

► *What are the main differences between men and women?*

The main differences show up in most girls after they are twelve and boys after they are thirteen. Women can have babies. Women's breasts develop and they can breast-feed their babies. Women menstruate. Men can father children with the sperm made in their testicles.

But as we think about it, men and women are more alike than different. Most men and women want to have a good education, find a job they like, have time for fun, make friends, fall in love with someone they would like to marry, have a nice family and be good citizens of the country in which they live.

► *How can a woman know if she's pregnant?*

In order for a conception to occur, sexual intercourse has to have taken place. (Exceptions are pregnancies produced by artificial insemination, in vitro fertilization and accidental entry of sperm ejaculated near the vagina.) A girl can get pregnant from having had intercourse only once. She will not have her menstrual period, although there can be some spotting. Usually, her breasts will become tender and slightly enlarged. Often she will feel nauseated and may vomit, especially in the morning. She will gain a little weight at the beginning. Some women have all of these signs right away, some have only one or two of them, some none. Any of these symptoms must be considered significant, and, if they occur, a pregnancy test should be done, preferably in a doctor's office.

► *What is incest?*

Incest occurs when two people who are closely related have sexual relations. It could be a father and daughter, a mother and son, or a brother and sister. Incest is illegal; both government and religion have forbidden incestuous relationships.

Children cannot marry parents, brothers and sisters cannot marry each other, and in many states cousins also are not allowed to marry. When they get older, most people meet and fall in love with someone they are not related to.

IN OUR WORDS

Here are some things children should know if they are nine, ten, eleven or twelve years old.

Human reproduction refers to the creation of a new person. After a female develops breasts and pubic hair and begins to menstruate, she can become pregnant if she has sexual intercourse with a developed male who produces sperm. Along with its capacity to become enlarged and harder, the penis, when stimulated, will at times release semen—a whitish, sticky fluid which contains sperm. About the same time a male's testicles begin to produce sperm he is also growing hair around the genitals, showing the first signs of whiskers and experiencing other physical changes (usually between the ages of eleven and fourteen).

If a sperm unites with the egg cell (called ovum) after sexual intercourse, it is called fertilization. If the fertilized cell attaches to the wall of the uterus, the female becomes pregnant.

Every month one egg matures and travels from one of the ovaries through the Fallopian tube toward the uterus. It can happen that two eggs mature at the same time. Both eggs can be fertilized as the result of sexual intercourse. They then become twins—either two male children, two females or one of each, male and female. These twins are each in their own amniotic sac. Their genetic makeup is not exactly the same. It is similar, though, since they have the same parents. They are called fraternal twins.

The other kinds of twins are called identical twins, and they are always of the same sex. Identical twins are created when a fertilized egg divides in half, and two separate fetuses then begin to develop. Since they came from the same egg and sperm, their genetic makeup is identical and they are in the same amniotic sac. Fraternal twins often look similar, but identical twins are often very hard to tell apart.

The female "period" is called menstruation. The period lasts for about five days each month. This occurs in females who are not pregnant. Blood-enriched tissue is released from the uterine walls through the vagina. So, when a female has a period, she wears a protective sanitary pad or tampon. This is for her comfort and to prevent her clothes from getting stained. Some women feel slightly ill or have cramps just before or during their periods, but most engage in regular activities. Their daily shower or bath should continue during that period so that body odor can be avoided.

The male "wet dream" is called a nocturnal emission. This happens to almost all boys. If not prepared, they think there is something wrong with them. What they have released is semen. It is natural for boys to dream and get excited about sexual thoughts. This causes the penis to get hard or erect. If excited enough, semen comes out. This is called ejaculation. ("Come" or "climax" are other terms used.)

Wet dreams continue for several years. They usually stop when males develop regular opportunities for sexual release, whether through masturbation or sexual intercourse.

In any case, wet dreams are perfectly normal. There is no need to try to control them; they happen to 99 percent of all boys. Without guilt, they can be an enjoyable experience—no matter how strange or sexy the accompanying dreams are. They are only slightly inconvenient, because the bedclothes do get wet and need changing. Parents realize this is a sign of a boy's normal growth.

MORE ON MASTURBATION

By the time children are ten to twelve years old, masturbation has become an important issue for them. (And, as we mentioned, it's often a big issue for the parents as well.)

Children can simply be told, "Masturbation is a big word for rubbing or stroking the penis, vulva and/or vagina. It's an enjoyable feeling for both boys and girls. Girls do not ejaculate, but they do lubricate, and at the height of pleasure they have an orgasm. (As with males, 'come' or 'climax' are other terms used.) No harm can come from doing it. However, like everything else that is pleasant, if it's done more than you really feel like it, it stops being a nice experience. For example, at any given time you may enjoy one ice cream cone, perhaps even two, but the third one makes you feel stuffed. Any good feeling should be treasured and not abused by making it routine or ordinary."

As noted by Mary Calderone, one of the main reasons many adults fail to achieve sexual satisfaction is interference by *their* parents with the discovery of their bodies as a source of pleasure.

CHAPTER SEVEN

What Children Need to Know: The Adolescent Years

O ur society often views adolescence as a disorder or a disease. It's seen as a traumatic period. Yet for many young people adolescence is a wonderful time of life. There are parents today who, when they look back on their earlier years, find that their adolescence was the period when they had the most fun, the most freedom and the best experiences of love.

We also know that adolescence can be a difficult time for some young people, either during its entire course or for brief, isolated periods. Problems encountered during adolescence, such as a teenager giving birth to a child, could adversely affect the remainder of the lives of both the parent(s) and the child. A significant number of individuals have lifelong troubles that originated in adolescence—delinquency, drug or alcohol abuse, premature parenthood, and a sense of alienation.

It is significant, too, that young people in our society have sex earlier and more frequently during their teenage years than in previous eras. A recent professional journal reported the results of two nationwide studies on teenage female sexuality conducted by researchers at Johns Hopkins University. These studies suggest that by age sixteen one in five teenage women has engaged in sexual intercourse. That means, of course, that 80 percent haven't had sex by age sixteen. By age nineteen, however, 66 percent have engaged in sexual relations. By age seventeen, one in ten has experienced at least one pregnancy. Again, that also means that 90 percent have not become pregnant. Yet if current increases in sexual activity continue, about 35 percent of adolescent females will have one or more pregnancies while still teenagers (before the age of twenty).

These trends affect a very significant portion of the population. It is easy to say that this can happen only to someone else, to a neighbor's child or to someone from a lower socioeconomic stratum. Unfortunately, many parents who think so are deceiving themselves. It is true that lower socioeconomic groups account for a higher percentage of teenage pregnancies, but sexual intercourse among teenagers is a widespread phenomenon now scattered throughout all social and economic classes in this country. Thus it is vitally important for the parents of today's growing generation to appreciate a few important ideas.

We cannot operate on the assumption that young people are knowledgeable about their own sexuality. Schools which sponsor sexuality education programs often postpone the instruction until after the young person has already begun to experiment with sex. Traditionally, parents themselves have exercised a relatively minimal role in sex education. You may want to review the following questions which, in our experience, are the twenty most frequently asked by teenagers. Consider how you might respond if approached with questions similar to these.

1. How can you tell if you are really in love?
2. Is it all right for people our age [fifteen, sixteen and seventeen] to have sex?
3. Is masturbation normal?
4. What causes a person to be homosexual? Is it normal?
5. Why is it easier for males to have sex without emotional involvement than for females?
6. How can a girl tell if she has an orgasm?
7. Do pot, alcohol or other drugs act as a sexual stimulant?
8. Is the pill harmful?
9. How can you tell if you have VD?

10. What is a good contraceptive to use if you are not having sex often?
11. Does the size of one's penis make a difference? How long is the average-size penis?
12. Is it normal if you don't feel ready to have sex?
13. Is it normal to use the mouth in sex play?
14. How come most parents don't tell their children about sex?
15. Can a girl become pregnant the first time she has intercourse?
16. Am I abnormal if I have thoughts about sex with people I know—like in my family?
17. Can I get birth control without my parents knowing about it?
18. How can one avoid pregnancy?
19. How come I get erections even when I'm not thinking about sex?
20. Is porno harmful?

When parents are not askable, young people invariably get their sex information—often misinformation—from their friends. There is a tremendous amount of sex education that occurs without parental awareness or consent in the lunchroom, the locker room, the bathroom, through graffiti, pornography, sex jokes and the boasts and bravado of some of the presumed sexually active young people.

Young people also receive a great deal of sexual information from movies and television, most of it of a sensationalistic and distorted nature. They need their parents' rational perspective to help counterbalance the distorted images all around them. Adolescents are aware of the local and national scandals reported almost daily in the press. Few people are naïve regarding a lot of "bad stuff" occurring in our lives. They sense the hypocrisy when adults establish themselves as models while, at the same time, these same adults are responsible for sexual exploitation in the media. There is little restraint used by television when it comes to exposing young people to the range of immorality extant in the world. We're not suggesting the imposition of censorship. Instead, we call upon television executives to be aware of the impressionable ages of many of their listeners and act more responsibly, especially in reducing the amount of gratuitous violence that predominates on prime-time network programming and, more recently, on cable. Although one can't directly connect the content of television programs with children's sexual development, it does appear to us in our clinical work that there is a brutalizing effect in the depiction of excessive violence, especially on boys, as expressed in a lack of sensitivity to the feelings of others and a persistent need to dominate. Indeed, this may be a major factor, as children become adults, in the increasing incidence of domestic violence.

The same networks that feature violence display little sense of responsibility in sexual education. There is virtually no educational programming for children and parents; and advertisements for contraceptives are not accepted, on the grounds of being "controversial" (i.e., some parents might object). There have been a few good TV documentaries, but the best "sex education" program, the Phil Donahue show, is not on prime time.

Advertisers use sex to peddle their wares. Barely clad women offer tubes of toothpaste, drape themselves over automobiles and project sales pitches for countless products and services.

Sex is also used to exploit teenagers in their own youth culture. The sexist lyrics of rock music as well as the Hollywood image of sexiness and success give ample testimony to this statement.

Society fails to appreciate the high price we pay for allowing the double standard to flourish. Earlier, we gave figures concerning the number of young girls who engage in sexual behavior. Most of these percentages are much higher for boys. In fact, current conservative estimates suggest that more than 60 percent of boys and 40 percent of girls will have had sexual intercourse before they leave high school. Boys are "expected" to have sexual intercourse. If they do not receive this message at home, they certainly get it from their peer group. Girls, on the other hand, are not even expected to be sexual, at least not until they are older or married.

Many families either explicitly or implicitly encourage this double standard. For example, a father will imply that it is okay for his son to have sexual experiences. Often there is a lot of kidding around which gives the impression that if the boy wants to be a man he is expected to be active sexually. Many parents do communicate to their sons that sex is ideally an expression of love and never a weapon to be used against anyone. We know many young men who act responsibly and with sensitivity because their parents were able to convey this message clearly and unequivocally. Those young men are less apt to succumb to peer pressure and do not feel a need to prove their masculinity through insincere sexual behavior. Conversely, almost all families, whether or not the parents were sexually active as teenagers, expect their daughters not to engage in sexual activities, or at least expect them to abstain from sexual intercourse until marriage.

This is precisely where the conspiracy begins. Parents mistakenly think their children will use restraint simply because their parents don't want them to engage in sex. Many parents refuse to respond to requests for birth-control information, thinking that if they give such advice their child will see this as permission to engage in sexual behavior. There is risk in everything; we believe that it is more of a risk *not* to talk to teenagers about their sexuality and birth control.

Parents who are waiting for the "right time" to sex-educate their adolescents may be endangering them more than they realize. Since a significant proportion of teenagers are experimenting with intercourse at fourteen, fifteen and sixteen, they clearly need concise information before they begin to do so. Recent research at Johns Hopkins indicates that adolescents are at greatest risk during the first few months of sexual activities; 22 percent of all out-of-wedlock births were found to result from intercourse during the first month after the first act of intercourse; fully 50 percent of all births to unmarried teenagers result from intercourse within the first six months of sexual activity.

The stakes are very high. Research reveals that less than 20 percent of sexually active teenagers use contraception of any form the first times they have sex. Only about 30 percent use some reliable form of contraception as they continue to have sexual relations. All too often we hear the ludicrous complaint made by some extremists that the pill, being the "easiest" form of contraception, is responsible for making girls promiscuous. Actually, use of the pill is unrelated to promiscuity. The sexual irresponsibility of most promiscuous girls is usually the result of a lack of understanding. Their parents have not informed them, or instilled in them a sense of sexual responsibility. These parents simply establish rules forbidding sex and assume that this is all there is to it.

Establishing rules is sometimes not a deterrent for actions. Teenagers will engage in sexual relations whether we like it or not and whether they like it or not. We say this quite deliberately. Most teenagers who engage in sexual intercourse don't even enjoy it. The girls virtually never have orgasms the first time they have sexual intercourse. Most boys who have sex as teenagers are more likely to have an orgasm when they tell their male friends about the experience than when they're actually having sex. Dr. Sylvia Hacker reported in her research on teenage contraceptive behavior that young people are indeed engaging in sex more and more and at younger and younger ages. However, she continues, while the activity is increasing, the comfort with which it is engaged in is not. The ignorance, guilt, fear and pressure accompanying the activity are enormous. It is simply without any vision of reality to operate on the assumption that young people will abstain just because we think they should.

History has wisely taught us to beware of how myths, fears and superstitions can influence the political arena. From fear of overstimulating young people or of "putting ideas into their heads that weren't there to begin with," we sometimes deprive them of knowledge that is vital to their well-being.

CULTURAL PRESSURES

If parents wish to understand their teenagers and help them through this difficult period in their lives, they would do well to reflect on the cultural and economic climate in which the young people are coming of age. Rapid changes in the social fabric during the post–World War II era have resulted in a confusion of cultural values and a demise of traditional social behavior. We live in a world that puts a premium on achievement and competitiveness. These values may be necessary components of industrial society, but they do cause emotional and psychological stress among adolescents who see them as incompatible with the ideals of love and caring that parents advocate. Society prizes educational achievement and claims that it holds the key to "success," which itself has become a one-dimensional issue of monetary gain. Simultaneously, alternate lifestyles have been downplayed, creating a standardization of behavior that adolescents often feel stifles individual self-expression. All this places an emotional strain on many adolescents.

Another cultural factor is the decline of religion as a guidepost for teenagers. We all seem to be victims of an age that encourages "instant gratification"—especially reinforced by the styles and fads of the youth culture. Trends among adults contribute equally: the nuclear family, in many instances, no longer provides the required socialization and disciplining functions. The intergenerational conflicts in sexual ethics that result from this breakdown often compound the sense of confusion. It is also vital for parents to perceive that many things have changed since their own teenage years and that values from their own childhood may no longer be dominant social forces.

Today's teenagers face not only changing cultural tides but biological ones as well. A century ago, the average age of first menstruation was seventeen; today it is twelve. The onset of fertility in boys (first ejaculation) has also been decreasing, and typically it occurs today between twelve and thirteen years of age. We cannot ignore the fact that physiologically it is more difficult for today's adolescents to wait until marriage, or until their twenties, to experience sexual intercourse. Today's adolescents not only mature earlier but delay marriage longer than the teenagers of generations ago.

Understandably, these changing tides have given rise to a new set of legends, such as the popular myth that most teenage females who become pregnant want to have babies, at least on an unconscious level. Virtually all research in this field is based on girls who are already pregnant and who decide to give birth. We have studied sexually active but not yet pregnant girls and found that less than 10 percent of teenage girls actually want to get pregnant.

In most cases, teenage girls become pregnant because of risk-taking, accidents or ignorance. We do not believe that ignorance is the only factor, although it provides a large component of the explanation for pregnancy; for instance, the majority of teenagers don't even know when in their cycle girls are most fertile. We also do not accept the conclusions drawn by some researchers that suggest parents are always at fault. Many parents are askable and do as good a job as possible in relating to their teenage children, yet their children engage in sexual intercourse, and in some cases their daughters or sons are involved in a pregnancy.

Several other myths pervade parents' thinking about their teenagers. It's commonly believed that first intercourse typically occurs in a car, when in fact it most often happens in the parents' home, or that of a friend. Parents of a young girl who matures physically before her peers tend to believe that this predisposes her to early sexual relations; actually, there is a relationship between early sexual experiences and growing up in poverty, but not early on the basis of puberty *per se*. Parents of a teenage boy who shows no interest in dating by age sixteen worry that he may be homosexual (no basis in fact). These and other legends illustrate the dangers of prejudging children based on misinformation.

VULNERABILITY

We need to understand teenage *vulnerability*, an important factor here. Vulnerability occurs not only because of membership in a discriminated-against single-parent family or minority group or due to poverty. There are members of such minority groups who are not vulnerable and who function very well in society. The same holds true for individuals who have been brought up in poverty. Young people feel vulnerable because of poor self-images—they feel they're not pretty, too short, too tall, too developed or not developed enough. These are bound to be common feelings when the body is manifesting many changes and when peers are developing at many different rates. Young people may also feel there is something wrong with them if their parents are divorced, or if they are adopted. Some adolescents feel vulnerable because they haven't had sex yet or even because they think it's wrong to feel sexual. Some feel vulnerable because of a physical or mental handicap. Thus, even in the "best" families—families that really care about their children—we can find children who, for a number of reasons, feel vulnerable, and vulnerable teenagers are the *most* prone to engage in irresponsible sexual behavior.

We're clear on what we mean by irresponsible behavior. It is careless, risk-taking sexual activity that could lead, for example, to pregnancy, STD or psychological trauma. In our judgment, most pregnancies among teenagers are the result of such irresponsible behavior. There are exceptions, but they are few and far between. Put simply, teenagers who feel inferior, inadequate or insecure—namely, vulnerable—are at greatest risk. Eleanor Roosevelt stated that "no one can make you feel inferior without your consent." We wish that we could impress this message on the hearts of all young people today.

The vulnerability of adolescence is not an indefinite state of affairs. Vulnerable periods can last for days or weeks and crop up at different periods of time. In general, those few young people whose difficulties persist over long periods live in circumstances in which their feelings of powerlessness are constantly reinforced. Statistically, perhaps 70 percent of teens manage quite well without major trauma. Though this fact doesn't minimize the plight of those teens who suffer from STD, pregnancy, emotional difficulties or drug abuse, it does caution us to proceed with an awareness that we must not treat all adolescents as if they were time bombs waiting to detonate.

In an ironic sense, adolescents suffer some anxiety and uncertainty from all the attention currently being focused on their sexuality. Statistics in the news, magazine articles and social commentators, though usually well-intentioned, have unwittingly helped blow teenage sex out of proportion. It can become both a self-fulfilling prophecy and a source of adolescent grievance. Because the accounts usually concern the perils of teenage sexuality—such as STD and pregnancy—the majority of teens, who are in fact responsible, sometimes resent the idea that they aren't trusted. Interestingly, in a recent study, teenagers stated that sex was not terribly important in their lives. The teens rated "having friendships with members of the same sex," "doing well in school," "having friendships with members of the opposite sex," "being very romantically involved with someone," and "athletics" as more important than "having sex with someone."

We must acknowledge that some young people who engage in sex with love and caring, and who use contraceptives, are mature. There are sixteen- and seventeen-year-olds who are more mature and capable than some adults, but they are the exceptions, and we still feel that teenagers should wait to experience sexual intercourse. It would, however, be unjust to write this chapter without acknowledging that mature adolescents do exist.

COMMUNICATION

If boys and girls openly and freely accept their sexual feelings, they will have questions to ask: Am I ready? What is the best method of birth control for me? If, however, they pretend that they are not sexual, but into idealized, romantic love, or a test of manliness or womanliness, then the important questions don't get asked. Parents who sense that their teenager is or will soon be sexually active have an obligation to bring up the subject of obtaining birth-control information. If, on the other hand, the teen asks about sex or birth control, don't assume he or she must be sexually active. It is essential that one be sensitive to the child's reason for asking.

In discussions of this nature, it is common for adolescents to put one parent in a dilemma by saying, "I'll tell you, but don't tell Dad [Mom] about it." The parent's response might be, "Okay, if that's how you want it, but I wonder if you'd let me use my own judgment here. You are putting me in a difficult situation." If the child insists, then you'll have to go along in order to gain the child's confidence. Once you do make such a promise, keep it *unless* it is a true emergency where you can't risk the consequences of keeping silent.

Parents need to be sensitive to the main worries that young people have. More often than not they are related to being liked or fitting in, making friends, having fun, pursuing interests, and elementary things like having "enough" spending money. In the sexual areas these worries are translated into an overall concern about being normal. Specifically, they focus on:

- Am I sexually attractive?
- Will I grow more?
- Why do my genitals seem so small or oddly shaped?
- Why am I so slow in developing (pubic hair, breasts, hips, deep voices, whiskers, etc.)?
- Will I ever find someone who will love me?
- Will anyone ever want to have sex with me (or will I ever have the courage to make a sexual overture)?
- Will everyone make fun of me if I admit I want to be a virgin on my wedding night?

Teenagers also have a very strong need for autonomy; this includes wanting parents to respect their differences of opinion. They need models, not critics. It is crucial for them to be helpful to others; this enhances their feelings of self-worth and achievement. *Perhaps of greatest benefit is teaching adolescents to accept one another.* Often their first experiences of love and relationships set the tone for future feelings and perceptions of the opposite sex as well as of themselves.

The double standard makes life extremely difficult for teenagers. Many young girls feel that they won't amount to anything unless some boy wants and loves them. Most don't realize that almost every boy who impregnates a teenage girl eventually abandons her. Even when teenage parents marry, the family is likely to break up, for one reason or another. It is a rare teenage couple burdened with an unintended pregnancy that remains intact after five years. We don't want to go into all the details regarding the repercussions of teenage motherhood, but here are a few facts American families should know.

A teenage girl basically has three options when she becomes pregnant. In general, the most traumatic of these options is having the baby, followed closely by giving the child up for adoption. The least residual trauma results from an abortion, though there are important exceptions to this generalization. We play no games on this subject. We clearly and unequivocally believe that if a teenager becomes pregnant, whether due to a mistake, a rape or a contraceptive failure, she should have the right to choose this third alternative. Incidentally, it is our position that any girl under fifteen is incapable of giving informed consent for sexual intercourse, no matter how sophisticated she may appear. This is legally the case in most states, and the offense is called statutory rape.

We respect the views of those who are opposed to abortion. You will follow your own conscience, but most of us *will* agree that abortion is not an appropriate form of birth control. In any case, the subject of abortion is not a simple matter, and we should all work toward eliminating the need for abortion in the first place.

Having stated our position regarding abortion, we would like to review briefly the consequences of a teenager's giving birth. Much poor health and psychological disturbance in our society is related to being born to or being a teenage mother. Low birth weight, infant mortality, physical disabilities and retardation are all common among babies born to teenagers. The chances of such children being physically abused or becoming delinquent or drug-addicted is much greater than if they are born to an older woman. The life script of a teenage mother is also grim. Her chances of finishing school, obtaining a good job or marrying someone who will be in the picture for more than a few years are minimal. In this context it seems almost trivial to point out that in the next twenty years the American taxpayer will pay in excess of $100 billion (at current prices) for the net results of teenage childbearing. Many of the 600,000 babies born each year to teenagers end up on the welfare rolls.

DECISION-MAKING

It is important for parents to understand the tremendous pressure on teenage girls to have sex. Boys use lines. A recent study conducted by Planned Parenthood in Chicago surveyed a thousand young men. They were asked if it was okay to lie to a girl, to say that you were in love with her in order to have sex. Seventy percent said yes!

Many girls are vulnerable to such lines because they don't admit they're having sex at all; they think they're "making love" and acting in a spontaneous and romantic way—and if one is spontaneous and romantic, one doesn't use birth control. To do so would suggest premeditated sex, which they have been taught is wrong. Girls are brainwashed, sometimes by their own parents, not to look upon themselves as sexual human beings. Hence they give no thought to the possible consequences of their actions, hoping instead that fate will be kind to them.

Ironically, few boys ever have sex spontaneously. They are planning, organizing and thinking about this for some time. Yet they are not immune to notions of romance or the spontaneity of the moment, nor are they free of ambivalence about their own sexuality. It cannot be too strongly emphasized that young people who know that strong sexual drives are normal and natural can better control their impulses and be more responsible in all areas of sexuality.

It was once thought that a disproportionately high number of pregnancies occurred among black teenage girls because *their* parents loved and wanted more children. This is simply not true. We have worked extensively with black families and have yet to meet parents who wanted their teenage daughter to become pregnant. We won't elaborate on the question of the acceptance of out-of-wedlock babies at this point, but we doubt that, in practice, there is a better level of acceptance in any particular racial, social or economic group.

It is difficult for most parents to deal with these sensitive issues. The strong sexual drives that confuse and delight their adolescent children may reawaken old fears and anxieties of their own. When we are lecturing to high-school classes, it is not unusual for a student to ask, "What you say is all well and good, but what do you do at the peak of passion?" Adults who are present invariably seem about to faint. Yet the youngster's question is a fair one. It can only be countered with: "What are you going to do when you're pregnant?" or "What are you going to do when you get someone pregnant?" One could add, "If you're at the 'peak of passion' and have reached a point of no return, why not consider an alternative to sexual intercourse, such as masturbation? It's satisfying and doesn't create any pregnancies."

When we ask parents, especially mothers of daughters, whether they would prefer their children to have sexual intercourse or to masturbate, often their response is that this is an unfair question. Why? We doubt there can be any significant reduction of irresponsible sexual behavior unless young people feel free to masturbate. For some parents, this is the most controversial statement we have made so far. People are sexual; why deny it? When young people say they're horny, they mean it. They feel sexual tension. They want relief. In our judgment, the best relief for sexual excitement and tension for teenagers is masturbation.

Teenagers involved in an intimate relationship often find that in the midst of kissing and heavy petting, sexual tensions become very intense; at those times it's nearly impossible, they say, to tell yourself, "Well, I can go home and masturbate later." Sometimes adolescents are not able to delay the impulse toward sexual release, and unfortunately this often leads to unplanned sexual intercourse. In these situations, mutual masturbation may be a realistic alternative. There is a risk in this, as it may progress to intercourse, but there is an even greater risk among those couples who move immediately to intercourse.

Sometimes we have been accused of giving contradictory messages. For instance, we state very clearly that we think sexual intercourse is good; yet we don't want teenagers to engage in it. (Here we are not referring to other forms of sexual expression in caring relationships, such as kissing, necking or mutual masturbation.) We think that young people should not engage in sexual intercourse until they are at least eighteen and off to college, working or living on their own. A person in his or her later teen years knows more, is more mature and can deal better with the consequences of even irresponsible behaviors. We see no contradiction here. One must reach a certain age to vote, drive a car or sign a contract. There are good moral and health reasons for parents to urge their children not to have sexual intercourse while they, the parents, are still in charge. After a child is employed or off to college, we can only hope (and pray) that our moral influence remains a vital force in their lives.

There are many types and degrees of sexual behavior. Some people are more sexual with each other when they hold hands or look into each other's eyes than when engaging in actual intercourse. There can be more sexual excitement in kissing or caressing than in the sexual act itself. In fact, much of what constitutes sexual intercourse is not even enjoyable for many young people because they don't have enough understanding of how to enjoy each other and to appreciate its deeper meaning. Often the motivation of having sexual relations is not for pleasure or intimacy, but for a false notion of self-respect: for boys, sex often means proving masculinity; for girls, desirability or femininity. As suggested by Gisela Konopka, "In our culture, success for a girl means being attractive and acceptable to boys."

There is a great deal of pressure put on adolescents to engage in sexual relations. Yet many we know who have "gone all the way" are among the most bored, alienated and unhappy young people you can imagine, drifting from one sexual partner to another. Sex without intimacy is rarely a satisfying experience. People make mistakes, experiment and have brief encounters, often unhappily. Adults should be able to cope with such emotional turmoil, but it can be very hard on children, even psychologically damaging. This is a large reason why, because of our experience, we say to adolescents that they shouldn't have sexual intercourse during their early teenage years.

It is sometimes tempting to believe that the pendulum is swinging back to more traditional ways of thinking. For instance, a recent Educational Communications (Lake Forest, Illinois) survey of top high-school students (those listed in "Who's Who Among American High School Students") reported that they were predominantly responsible and conservative in their sexual attitudes. Seventy-six percent said they had not had sexual intercourse, and only 8 percent said they favored couples living together before marriage. Such elitist groups do tend to be more knowledgeable about sex, and they are generally less vulnerable than the average student. The study substantiates our view that informed adolescents delay their first sexual intercourse until after high school.

However, studies suggest there is a significant turnaround once these students go to college. A survey of 325 students at a state college in Kentucky (53 percent freshmen, 18 percent sophomores, 13 percent juniors, 16 percent seniors) showed that 67.4 percent had experienced intercourse and 31.7 percent had not; 0.9 percent did not respond. A similar survey of 420 Syracuse University students (0.9 percent freshmen, 29.9 percent sophomores, 16 percent juniors, 48.8 percent seniors, 1.9 percent graduates, 2.5 percent no response) indicated that 82 percent had experienced intercourse and 15 percent had not; 3 percent gave no reply. Both studies, which were carried out in the spring of 1979, also revealed no significant differences in sexual behavior among those who identified themselves as Catholic, Protestant or Jewish. There were many more upperclassmen in the Syracuse sample, which probably explains why a higher percentage had experienced intercourse.

BETWEEN PARENTS AND CHILDREN

The most important message we have for parents is this: Let your children know that no matter what they do, you will never reject them. The most responsible message you can give is, "You are our child; no matter what happens you can come to us and we'll help you."

Some of you may remember the furor created in 1975 when former First Lady Betty Ford said, "I do not believe in premarital relationships, but I realize that many in today's generation do not share my views. However, this must never cause us to withdraw the love, the counseling and the understanding that they may need now more than ever before." She created a media sensation when she acknowledged the possibility that her daughter might choose to have premarital sex, but when it was more soberly reviewed, the vast majority of the American public appreciated what she had said. Most ministers endorsed her position. Here is a good example of how the media can overreact; they created the impression that Mrs. Ford's statement was permissive and somehow dangerous.

We endorse the openness and honesty of Betty Ford's statement. It demonstrates a sense of caring and respect between parent and child that is critical. Parents who communicate their confidence in their children to work out their own particular values find generally that it is the parents' important values they select in the end. Parents who take an uncompromisingly harsh position devoid of mutual trust are inviting tragedy. Nearly a million teenagers run away from home each year in this country. Girls account for almost half this number; as many as 40 percent of them do so because they are pregnant. When interviewed later, they make statements such as "My father said that if I ever became pregnant he'd kill me" or "My mother said that if I ever became pregnant I shouldn't come home." These runaways face horrors that are simply beyond belief. Many end up the victims of pimps who immediately turn them into prostitutes. It may also be appropriate to add that pregnancy is reliably reported to be the most prevalent reason for suicide among teenage girls.

Even parents who have good relationships with their offspring often reach an impasse when it comes to speaking openly and freely about sexuality. Perhaps they regret not having spoken to their youngsters sooner, and now that they want to make up for this deficiency their children remain unresponsive. Sometimes one can grasp a good opportunity—an article in the newspaper, a dinner-table conversation about advice that Dear Abby, Ask Beth or Ann Landers has given—and make this into a teachable moment. Your child may not respond, but at least he or she is listening to the conversation. You might bring home a well-illustrated sexuality education book and just leave it on the coffee table. The child will no doubt become curious.

It must also be made clear here that teenagers are entitled to privacy. They should not be expected to tell parents everything. This can be painful to caring parents who feel they can be of little help if their teenagers don't reveal the intimacies and intricacies of their lives. Sometimes teenagers kid around to mask what really happens, and others report that they tell their parents what they assume the parents want to hear.

Sometimes parents who genuinely mean well lose their children's confidence by the way in which they express themselves. Here is a list of phrases guaranteed to turn off young people:

- I want to have a serious talk with you.
- We trust you.
- When I was your age . . .
- Because we say so.
- As long as I don't know about it.
- Act your age.
- It's about time you . . . (got good grades, straightened your room).
- Just a minute.
- Ask your father/mother.

- Are you telling me the truth?
- That's not your idea, is it?
- Don't you dare talk to me that way.
- Get off your high horse.
- Wipe that smile off your face.
- What will the neighbors say?
- After all we've done for you . . .

Parents need to be especially careful when a youngster says that he or she is in love. Your initial reaction might be to respond in one of the following ways. "You'll get over it." "When you get older you'll laugh about it." "It's puppy love." Never slight a young person experiencing (or thinking he or she is experiencing) love. One should worry about the relationship only if inappropriate behavior is associated with it, such as not doing school homework. It might be helpful for you as parents to read the section for teenagers on how to tell when you are really in love (pages 144–46). You'll thus be able to help your child make distinctions between mature and immature love.

It is not easy to give advice about what to do if your child insists on dating earlier than you think is appropriate. One approach is to just validate your youngster's feelings even as you refuse the demands. Hold to your principles and don't allow your young teenager to sway you with comments that you are old-fashioned or that all the other kids in the neighborhood have more permissive parents. Acknowledge that you may be different (or old-fashioned or too strict, etc.) from their friends' parents, but don't get caught debating your own parental qualifications.

There are, however, many situations in the lives of teenagers which are not subject to parental control. The following incident actually happened to an acquaintance of ours. A seventeen-year-old girl called her mother late at night and told her that she was with her boyfriend and they had been drinking quite a bit. It was too late for her to get public transportation, and the boyfriend offered to take her home on his motorcycle. Our friend did not drive and in her anxiety did not think of an alternate solution such as a taxi. She responded by telling the daughter to stay overnight; she admitted later that she preferred to have her daughter pregnant to having her dead. We all must use common sense in some situations, even though it may violate our principles.

While we have stressed the importance of knowledge throughout this book, we want to affirm that it is no guarantee of intelligent behavior. Most people have read the Surgeon General's warning about the smoking of cigarettes and the risk of lung cancer, yet many intelligent people do smoke. In the same vein, decisions about sex are not necessarily tied to knowledge. Even knowledgeable adults sometimes engage in irresponsible sexual behavior. We still insist that with knowledge there is *generally* more responsible behavior than without it, but knowledge by itself is not sufficient.

Feelings and levels of emotional maturity often are more important than knowledge. Providing information *per se* is not the main point in being an askable parent; one must also be able to identify with children and their feelings. Teenagers in general express a wide range of emotions. "I don't feel good about myself and won't until I have a boyfriend [girlfriend]." "I'm mortified because everyone is having sex and I'm the only one who isn't." We sometimes forget that we need to support young people who don't want to have sex. As you might recall, more than half of the teenage female population will not have sex during the high-school years and the same is true for about 40 percent of the boys.

We suggest providing guidelines for your children rather than rigid rules, which are often broken, either secretly or defiantly. How many families believe, for example, that if a teenager is home before midnight no sexual activity can take place? Do families understand, as do teenagers, that one certainly can have sex before midnight as well as after this arbitrary hour? It might be useful to talk over such an issue with your son or daughter. Make it clear that your main concern in having your child home at a reasonable hour is your worry about the possibility of muggings, robberies, accidents as a result of drunken driving, all of which do occur more frequently after midnight. Explain that you simply have a hang-up—you can sleep better knowing your child is safe at home. Children sometimes must be made responsive to their parents' needs. It makes sense to discuss these rules in advance.

Many parents are confronted with the dilemma of having a teenager return home from college with a lover and want to sleep with the lover during the visit. Many parents accept the situation, but those who disapprove must examine the consequences of their various responses. To threaten to do something extreme, such as cutting off college tuition, could result in a complete severance of family ties. If you are uncomfortable with the idea because of younger children, or for moral or religious reasons, it is naturally your right to forbid sharing a bed in your home. Before making your decision, however, you may wish to consider things from the young people's perspective. "We're sleeping together at school," they reason, "so why pretend at home that the situation doesn't exist?" If that sensible question sometimes seems defiant, it is probably because behind it lies an honest plea for parental acceptance of their sexuality. We believe that, in most cases, granting that acceptance can only improve family relationships.

To date, there is no evidence that living together sets the stage for unhappy marriages or divorce. In fact, if our own son came home and announced he wanted to marry a girl on relatively short acquaintance, we can imagine ourselves saying, "Why don't you live together first and get to know each other?" In any event, it is best to balance your own beliefs with an open responsiveness to your child's choice, rather than worrying about neighbors, relatives or anyone else.

Parents must also realize that it is natural for teens to take risks and make mistakes. Adolescence is a time for testing relationships and personal abilities. Teenagers test reactions to their behavior and try to decide on personal interests and goals, balancing them with the opportunities they perceive in society. The situation is critical only when they don't learn from these trials and errors along the way.

Both of us recently reread Hermann Hesse's *Siddhartha*, a book that was important to us when we were growing up. Hesse concludes his book with an observation that all parents would do well to remember: "Knowledge can be communicated, but not wisdom." Ultimately, as parents and a society, we need to give teens more support for their own stated priorities, dreams and ambitions. While we are doing this, we can empathize with young people and say we understand the pressures to engage in sexual intercourse, pressures which often push them away from their dreams. But at the same time we might say, "All right. We know that you are under pressures, that rock-music lyrics encourage you to have sex, but let me ask you: When you get pregnant, are you going to get a letter of congratulations from your favorite rock star? When you need an abortion, is Mr. Calvin Jeans going to send you the money?"

We have to let these young people know that their mothers aren't going to take care of their babies: "You've got a lot of nerve! Your poor mother? Why should she take care of your baby? That's not fair."

LETTERS FROM TEENAGERS

We receive a lot of letters from adolescents who have read one of the authors' books or attended a lecture. The letters often pose problems that the teens are having difficulty coping with, or discuss situations in which they feel hard pressed to maintain the integrity of their beliefs. We thought it would be enlightening for readers of this book to read about some teen concerns, in the words of teens themselves.

DEAR DR. SOL GORDON,

I read your book, "You Would If You Loved Me," and really enjoyed it . . . me and all of my friends, we've all been through breaking up because we wouldn't give him the main thing he wanted. Our hearts were all, of course, broken, and we even regretted (a little) not doing that, but we all know it was for the better.

Me and my boyfriend were together for 10 months and broke up for (mostly) that reason (sex!?). I always told him near the beginning of our relationship that he had better break up with me if he wanted to do that, but he'd always tell me that that wasn't what he wanted. He always wanted a fun relationship, so we just kept on going!!

But during the relationship he'd always try to pressure me in doing that, but I would always have excuses, or get mad at him, or remind him of the things that we had talked about earlier. Some of my excuses were: that I had my period; I had to be home at 12:00, and if I was late dad would kill both of us; that none of my other friends had done it and I didn't want to be the first one; and also just plainly say "no"!!! He'd of course get mad at me but it was mostly his fault that I would have to leave him in that state of "hard-on."

I would always try to tell him that we could have fun with each other and not have to do that. Because it's true: "If you really care for me and love me and love this relationship then you shouldn't pressure me, because none of this would be worth it or just be wasted if we had to break up for this dumb reason!!" So, I guess we did break up, and we are (kind of) good friends now. But from what I've heard, he still hasn't done that yet so he might just give up!

Mr. Gordon,

A couple of weeks ago two guys invited my girlfriend and I to a party. The whole night this one guy kept trying to get me to have sex with him, so I thought I'd write and tell you his lines. First of all, he kept trying to get me high all night, constantly lifting a beer to my lips and offering me a joint to smoke—he was trying to get me so high that I couldn't say "no." Then he started asking me if I wanted to go back to his place (he was three years older than me.)

He kept trying to kiss me and put his hands on my boobs, and I finally just told him "no sex." The last thing I remember of that terrible evening was that he said even though I didn't let him do anything that I was the nicest girl he'd ever been with. I wondered how many other girls he'd said that to! I was afraid he was going to rape me, and I finally got away by faking being sick from all the beer. Why are some guys so pushy they're willing to practically sit on top of you to get what they want?

Mr. Gordon,

I'm a 13-year-old girl, and my problem is this really cute guy who goes to my school. I fell in love with him, and one night we really started making out at his parents' place. Since then we have done *everything* but go all the way. We'll both be naked, and he will *beg* and *beg* me to go all the way. I'm too young to get pregnant and I don't know how to use any type of birth control. I want to be the one responsible for it. Also, we have to sneak and hide, which you said in your book was a no-no. Once my dad found out I had been over there, and he called me a slut, whore, etc. And he doesn't even know what happened. I really hate sneaking around, and my dad will throw me out if he finds out. Is it a line when you tell the guy "no" and he cries?

DEAR SIR:

I am a 15-year-old male from Michigan, and I have just finished reading your "lines" book *You Would If You Loved Me.* I had no idea that guys were only after sex, or were so lustful. It surprised me that it was the guys' fault for the 1,000,000 adolescent pregnancies. I think that more emphasis should be placed on the word "no." Every girl should know this. I have always thought that there's no excuse for getting a girl pregnant, but it seems like you are trying to lay down a guilt trip on the males of the world. I'm not saying that it's the girl's fault either. The responsibility should be a mutually shared and wanted satisfying adventure. I can't understand it being anything else.

DEAR DR. GORDON:

Could you give me some advice? I am a junior in high school here in New York, and I am a Christian. I have very fundamentalist values toward the subject of sex, and feel that people should wait until marriage. I believe God wants it that way. But that's my opinion.

I am now dating a young Christian man who I really love. We've discussed sex, and we're both virgins. A couple of days ago he told me that he wants to make love to me, and wants to wait for the right time. Dr. Gordon, I'm having trouble trying to remain in my virgin status. I would like to make love to him too, but I feel deep down that I'd sorely regret it. What if it hurt our relationship, or I don't marry him eventually? I want to be a virgin for my husband—what if I get hurt? Birth control is not the problem—the problem for me is a matter of religious values. Please help! I care enough for him to give up my virginity, but I still have these doubts.

DEAR DR. SOL,

. . . Well, to get to the real problem. I'm a sophomore in high school, and I have a hang-up about sex. Not your average teenage "oh isn't he a hunk." At dances and other places when I see a boy I like I go after him, and I really have had a lot of sexual relations. I have a terrible reputation. But I consider myself to be fairly intelligent—I just can't help it. I don't have any friends, except for these guys that come to see me for "favors." I tell myself to stop doing it, but I can't seem to—it's compulsory. My parents don't know anything about it, so please don't tell them I'm this way. But they're beginning to suspect. Please help me!

P.S. I hope you don't think this is a joke.

In concluding the chapter, we'd like to summarize our main messages to young people.

1. Girls get pregnant because they have sexual intercourse.
2. It's not romantic to have sex without birth control, it's stupid.
3. When someone says, "If you really love me, you'll have sex with me," it's *always* a line.
4. Sex is never a test or proof of love.
5. Sex is never a test or proof of masculinity or femininity.
6. "No" is a perfectly good oral contraceptive.
7. More than 85 percent of all boys who impregnate teenage girls will eventually abandon them.
8. Girls who feel they don't amount to anything unless some boy loves them should realize that self-worth never comes from someone else.
9. People who feel good about themselves tend to be more responsible in their sexual behavior.
10. Of the ten most important things in a relationship, sex is number nine. Number one is love and caring.

CHAPTER EIGHT

Parents' Questions About Adolescence

*I*t is during their children's adolescence that many parents have the most difficulty understanding, and responding to, sexual issues. In effect, living through their children's adolescence revives memories and feelings parents retain of their own teenage years, so that they essentially relive (vicariously through their children) their own adolescence. Fears, joys, painful remembrances are jolted from musty memory banks and often make it all the more difficult to deal effectively with the present.

DISCIPLINE AND RULES

A matter of critical importance for many families is how to handle authentic differences of opinion between the parents about management of their child. This is especially important in the area of sexuality because the consequences could be serious. Differences between parents can range from when to allow a child to go out on a date to an appropriate curfew time, to attitudes on how to handle male and female children. These differences can degenerate into real conflicts, which might start out as an accusation such as "You're too hard on the children" or "You don't trust the children enough." Not only can this have serious consequences for the marital relationship, but also the child may exploit the difference of opinion for his or her own benefit.

It is imperative that parents work through these conflicts and present a unified front. Sometimes one can take a flexible approach and say, "Listen. Your father [mother] and I disagree, but for now we're going to go with my point of view. If that doesn't make sense, in six months [or a year] we'll consider another alternative." Not all families are open to this kind of compromise, and parents may prefer to negotiate privately without informing the child of the process involved. Sometimes it's even worth doing a little research in the library; we're not suggesting that experts know it all, but sometimes you can get some good ideas that apply to your own situation. In some families it's even possible to have a family conference at which grievances are aired and solutions shared. Allowing a young person to negotiate within predetermined limits can foster excellent self-esteem and be a helpful preparation for adult life.

In any case, one must remember that the risk to the child is less serious when parents agree on management, even if somewhat misguided, than if they are constantly disagreeing or involving the child in subterfuge. The annals of child therapy are filled with stories in which one parent and a child align themselves against the other parent. Such conspiracy will tend to exacerbate the child's symptoms. Therapy usually aims to align the parents with each other and return the child to the child's role.

We discourage parents from involving the child in parental battles of will, no matter how minor they may seem. Even joking remarks such as "That's the way women are" or "All men are the same" can be harmful. Be aware that conflicts over a child can camouflage conflicts that really exist in the marriage. In these situations, parents "choose" to fight over a child rather than face the difficulties that exist between themselves.

Here are some parents' questions on discipline and rules, and our answers to them.

▶ *I'm a father whose seventeen-year-old son demands to know why I keep trying to influence him by setting rules for his behavior when, he argues, he's "grown-up." I'm not* really sure how to answer him, and this has become a real conflict between us.

You've raised a good question, and we're sure that parents of fourteen- and fifteen-year-olds have heard similar arguments from their children. Parents sometimes intuitively know that they need to enforce discipline within the family, but are stymied when asked their rationale for doing so.

Parents can tell their children, "It's important to us that you become a healthy, happy adult. That's why we say no alcohol or drugs, because these things interfere with psychological development. We want you home at night by a reasonable time so that you can get the sleep you need and we know you're not in danger. We also say no sexual intercourse, because it's too much of a risk to yourself mentally and physically. We feel that as long as you still live with us it's our responsibility to help you, to protect you." (At times you may have to add, "Whether you like it or not.")

▶ *I'm the mother of a fifteen-year-old son, and I feel that in the area of sex my son is particularly vulnerable and may be getting himself into some trouble. How can I express my concern for him without revealing the mistakes I feel I've made in my own life in the past?*

Even conservative parents reach adulthood with the feeling that they have made some mistakes in their past relationships and sexual behavior. They fear, on the one hand, being untruthful if they fail to divulge these experiences to children, and, on the other hand, being labeled hypocritical when they tell children to "do as I say, not as I did."

In this situation, a balance is important. It's not appropriate, or even advisable, to let children know the intimate details of your sexual life, good or bad. Presumably, that's one of the reasons why we're parents—we want to profit from the mistakes we've made and encourage our children to lead a better life than we've had. If we've learned from our mistakes, we don't see withholding information as hypocrisy at all. Acknowledging that you've made mistakes, and will continue to make them, is not an open invitation to be specific about the details.

This raises the question of how specific parents should be in setting sexually related standards for children. A conservative parent and colleague of ours, Alison Deming, surprised herself immensely when she one day told her son, "Don't ever knowingly use your penis as a weapon to hurt somebody." After she recovered from her shock at being so candid with her son, she found that the resulting conversation was one of the most rewarding ever. Somehow or other, girls are told that they need to protect themselves, but we neglect to give similar messages to boys.

Some parents, especially fathers, go so far as to imply that there might be something wrong with the teenage son who is still a virgin at sixteen or seventeen. This message is often conveyed in jokes and bawdy stories about "what hell-raisers we were when we were growing up." Boys benefit from the same information regarding self-control, discipline and responsibility as girls do.

▶ *What is your position on parental notification in cases where minor children seek prescription contraceptives or other medical services?*

It is natural and desirable for parents to want to know about important events and developments in their children's lives. Ideally this occurs in the context of loving parent–child relationships in which important issues are open for discussion. There are, however, many families in which such communication does not take place. The question arises: in instances where teenagers obtain birth-control help from clinics, is it justifiable or desirable for the clinic to notify the parents, with or without the minor's consent?

We believe that the health and welfare of the child must take precedence over other considerations. A 1982 survey of young patients at federally funded family-planning clinics reported in *The New York Times* suggested that 25 percent of these patients would stop applying for prescription contraceptives if their parents were notified. Only 2 percent said they would stop sexual activity as the result.

The New York Times further reported that no contraceptive

method affects a teenager's health more adversely than does pregnancy; teenagers are five times more likely to die from pregnancy-related causes than from use of the pill.

It is sad but true that Congress can legislate neither family solidarity nor responsible behavior. We believe that adolescents must be allowed to protect their health whether or not they choose to listen to good counsel. We must also remember that today's teenagers didn't create the "sexual revolution"—they are its victims.

PHYSICAL MATTERS

► *My daughter approached me with a question recently, and I'm not sure I handled it very well. She had been reading a book on sexuality addressed to young teens, and was especially concerned about first intercourse and the role of the hymen. She has always been athletic, and was worried that her hymen might have ruptured in vigorous exercise. I wasn't sure how to describe the hymen or how to find it, and I'm wondering if there was some underlying message in her question.*

Your question highlights the serious concerns which young teenagers have in relation to sexual intercourse and the various aspects of sexual expression. The hymen is no longer prized as a symbol of virtue (although for some couples the bride's virginity is significant to their marriage).

As your daughter suspected, exercise can break the hymen so that it is no longer there at first intercourse. Some females are born with a small or undetectable hymen, while in others it is pronounced. Through the use of tampons, or through masturbation, the hymen is sometimes broken.

Women who reach first intercourse with an intact hymen are sometimes concerned about painful penetration of the penis. Great gentleness on the part of the male is urged, along with some lubrication. Some bleeding may occur, and this is perfectly normal. Due to these circumstances and general inexperience, first sexual intercourse is not very enjoyable for many people.

You might tell your daughter that it's unwise for her to engage in sexual intercourse while still a teenager. As an adult, she'll be better able to make her own decisions concerning pre-marital sexual experiences. The important aspect here is not the hymen itself, but rather the love and caring between herself and her future partner, and the compatibilty of their values and goals.

This question also gives us an opportunity to address other fears which both boys and girls have about first sexual experiences. Boys worry whether they will be able to find the girl's vagina, whether they will be able to penetrate, and whether their penis will remain erect. Girls worry that they may appear clumsy, or will not have an orgasm. These "performance" anxieties again focus mistakenly on the mechanics of sex rather than on the partners' feelings and the meaningful aspects of the relationship.

Parents can help their children sort through these feelings to anticipate sexual intercourse as adults and in the process come to a better understanding of themselves, other people and the nature of sexuality in general. While a girl of your daughter's age should not be *sexually active*, it is good for her to be *intellectually and emotionally* prepared so that sex and intimate relationships do not come to her, later in life, as painful surprises.

► In this age of conformity, popularity and good looks, how do parents comfort children who don't feel themselves to be sexually attractive, let alone accepted by a peer group? We have a daughter who is fourteen years old, is small for her age, and has a severe case of acne. She is so troubled by her feelings of inferiority, especially in relation to boys, that even her ordinarily good grades are beginning to suffer.

We're sure we'd look foolish if we tried to offer a simple answer to this question. This is an age in which cliques and exclusive friendship groups dominate. It is also a time when children can be cruel to one another. We hate to say it, but sometimes the best thing is simply to help your child sweat it out. This goes for a wide variety of situations in which children are not popular for one reason or another: the handicapped (see also Chapter 11), the unattractive, those who appear to possess characteristics of the opposite sex.

We're specifically advocating that you at least help your child have a good relationship with you, her parents. Don't lie to the child and say, "If only you would try harder, everything would be all right," or "The only thing that counts is a good personality." Empathize with the child, suggesting that you know how difficult it is, but that you also know that as she gets older her intellectual and personality development will in fact become more important than her acned appearance, which indeed may well have been cured. She may not believe it, but you have to. This is a time when you may want to spend more time with her in terms of arranging activities, even if they are with relatives, as well as time spent within the family itself. We recommend the development of hobbies and special interests which exploit the individual's talents.

MASTURBATION

► *I'm a forty-two-year-old mother whose son is now fourteen. Often when I knock on his door, it takes him a long time to answer, and he occasionally spends a lot of time in the bathroom. I'm sure he's masturbating a lot, and despite all I've read about masturbation being "healthy," I can't seem to shake the feeling that it's wrong. Should I talk with my son about this?*

This sounds more like a personal dilemma rather than a specific conflict or problem between yourself and your son. What you say is true—it is difficult to overcome the childhood conditioning which taught us that masturbation is bad or to be feared. We appreciate your courage and openness, and would like to make some comments you might find helpful.

Adolescents can be helped to appreciate that masturbation is a healthy, normal way of expressing and enjoying their sexual feelings and relieving sexual tensions. Furthermore, why shouldn't adults be able to masturbate comfortably and pleasurably when opportunities for sex with their partners are not available?

Society pays a big price for its repressive views on masturbation. Clinical data and research on persons who have committed violent sexual crimes strongly suggests a relationship between feelings of guilt and punishment for childhood masturbation and the need to dominate or violate women or children. These symptoms also seem to go along with early parental rejection or deprivation.

Society has so brainwashed young men that many feel it's unmanly to masturbate once they've experienced sexual intercourse. Consequently, our country has left a sad reservoir of unwanted children in such places as Japan, Vietnam and Thailand. To many men, prostitution, or even rape, seem preferable to masturbation. This is no small matter.

Two brief anecdotes will illuminate the ways in which misperceptions continue to inhabit people's attitudes:

An editor of a medical journal asked us to respond to a question posed by a seventeen-year-old boy who stated that he couldn't speak to a female or go to a dance without getting an erection. The young man had pleaded for help. He especially asked that no one make fun of him; it was a serious matter for him. He also didn't want to be told that he'd get over it—which, the editor revealed, was the answer several experts offered nonetheless. We suggested to the young man that he simply masturbate before he went to a dance or had a date. If he felt it was necessary, he could repeat the process during the course of the evening. He should then be able to enjoy a relaxed night out without embarrassment. The editor refused to print our reply, claiming that it was not "professional" advice; we, however, still can't think of a better solution. The unpredictability of erections can be a great source of anxiety for young men. With masturbation, a boy can gain a reassuring sense of self-mastery and control.

Ten years ago one of us spoke before the mental-health association in an upstate New York community. Reference was made to masturbation. A reporter present accurately recorded what had been said. When the article was submitted to the editor, he refused to use the word "masturbation," since he felt that this was inappropriate terminology for a "family" newspaper. A debate then ensued among the staff members regarding a proper substitute for the word. Two were considered: "self-abuse" and "self-pleasuring." It was to the staff's credit that they finally agreed to use "self-pleasuring."

The treatment of choice for preorgasmic women involves learning how to enjoy self-pleasuring. Often women who have been preorgasmic for many years achieve their first orgasms through masturbation and then go on to become orgasmic with their partners as well.

For some people with sexual problems, masturbation can be a therapeutic tool where psychotherapy alone has failed. Men who suffer from premature ejaculation or impotence often learn greater control by using masturbation. In the last few decades, attitudes concerning masturbation have done a dramatic about-face among professionals, and these enlightened views are gradually filtering into the population at large.

Sure, we've come a long way. Woody Allen stated in one of his films that he enjoys masturbation—at least he's having sex with someone he loves. Some religious groups still frown upon it, yet even the most extreme opponents in the Catholic Church, for example, have modified their position considerably during the last twenty-five years. The book *Sexual Morality: A Catholic Perspective*, by the conservative theologian Philip S. Keane, provides ample testimony to this fact. We predict that twenty-five years from now no one will give masturbation another thought, except to acknowledge its pleasurable aspects.

Regardless of such idealistic prophecies, some parents will remain uncomfortable with masturbation, but the chain of anxiety can be broken by teaching your children to understand and accept their sexual impulses. Parents may not like to use words such as "masturbation" or expressions such as "playing with yourself." We're indebted to our colleague Gloria Blum for the concept of "private touching." It rightly suggests that masturbating, like other forms of sexuality, is not a public matter.

Our overall position is as follows: There is no evidence that all healthy people masturbate, or that you must masturbate to be healthy. Once may be too much if you don't enjoy it. There are people—especially some adult women—who have no memory of ever masturbating and who suffer no apparent ill effects. Some mature men and women give up masturbation entirely after they obtain regular opportunities for sexual intercourse; others enjoy masturbation more than coital sex. Most people continue to masturbate at some time or other throughout their entire lives.

In effect, we're suggesting that your concern about your child's "problem" is more than likely an indication of your own inhibitions. Masturbation should be a concern only when it is compulsively performed, and then it is a symptom of some other difficulty—in the same way that overindulgence in food and alcohol are symptoms of anxiety in other areas of a person's life. (People don't get drunk because they are thirsty.)

It is the responsibility of the parent to make sure that children understand that masturbation in private is normal. Beyond that, the parent should make judgments as to whether or not the child is adjusting or experiencing difficulty according to such criteria as (1) does he/she have friends, (2) does he/she make constructive use of leisure time, and (3) is he/she reasonably respectful to the family—that is, neither constantly rebellious nor overcompliant?

DATING

▶ *My fifteen-year-old daughter announced that she was going on a date with a boy she met that afternoon. (My daughter said she was going to go with him whether I liked it or not, and she's been in such a depressed, angry mood lately that I'm sure she would disobey me if I forbade it.)*

Let us tell an actual story of what one parent did in response to this situation. When Mrs. Jones realized that her daughter was going to go out with this young man anyway (the mother–daughter relationship had been deteriorating for some months), she stated that she didn't approve of it, but realized that there was nothing she could do. She extracted one commitment: the boy must come to the house and pick the girl up personally. When the young man came, Mrs. Jones invited him into the kitchen privately, saying, "I'd like to talk to you for a minute." She asked him if he had a driver's license. He said yes, and she asked him to produce it. At this point, Mrs. Jones copied down the name, address and license number and said to the young man, "You seem like a fine young man, but I think you can understand why I have reservations about my daughter, who is only fifteen, going out with you" (the young man was eighteen). "My daughter is determined, and there's no way I can stop her, so I want you to know that if she isn't home by eleven o'clock I will call the police immediately. Enjoy and have a good time."

When the daughter returned at ten-thirty, the mother asked if she had had a good time and she answered, "Not really. From about nine-thirty on, he kept asking what time it was. I guess you were right; I didn't like him that much anyway."

And that was that.

The whole issue of dating is a very complicated one. It's easy enough for us to state what seems appropriate, but obviously the follow-through is much more difficult. Children reach a point in their lives where they're testing us. Perhaps the most difficult problem is the presumption young people make that we are the most conservative, most old-fashioned, perhaps meanest parents that exist. Virtually all parents face this dilemma. Yet caring parents know they are entitled to establish rules, however unfair they seem to the child.

Having an adult present at a party attended by children under eighteen years of age should be a minimal expectation. Group dates rather than individual dates are preferred for younger teen-agers. We sometimes fail to appreciate that this is often a great relief to the young people themselves. Though peer pressure seems to encourage individual dating, young people themselves want the security of other people present.

Curfews need to be established, with an absolutely clear state-ment that no matter what happens the child must call if there's some reason for a late homecoming. The very best thing is for parents to establish contacts with one another, such as a simple telephone call saying, "My son is going to take out your daughter [or my daughter is going out with your son]. I just wanted you to know my telephone number." This as well as other social amenities, including a meeting with the other parents if the rela-tionship develops, will allow you to establish limits for your child's activities.

"Don't you trust me?"—that is a difficult question most ado-lescents constantly pose. A simple response is, "Of course we do, but we still have to take precautions that represent your best interests, whether they seem rational to you or not, and whether you like it or not." Another typical complaint is, "Oh, Mom/ Dad, you're treating me like a baby." The best response is, "I'm sorry it feels that way to you, but I still have to use my best judgment. That's what families are all about. If it turns out that I'm wrong, I'll certainly apologize."

A crucial dilemma that parents face is the possibility their children will engage in sexual intercourse at too young an age. Though they acknowledge that a child is entitled to privacy and a certain degree of free choice, they rightly want to protect the child from rash mistakes, such as pregnancy and sexually transmitted disease, to say nothing of the psychological problems related to premature sexual encounters. Both boys and girls are at risk here, but unfortunately even we must recognize that girls suffer the most for three reasons: (1) the girl is the only one who gets pregnant; (2) girls are often asymptomatic with respect to STDs (the boy usually knows he has it); and (3) in our "sexist" society, the girl often has sex because of the possibility of love, but the boy usually has sex because of the likelihood of sex—no small matter, however much we favor responsible behavior for both sexes.

Some parents have a hard time recognizing that you can talk to children about sexuality without giving them the impression you are proposing that they have sex. Here is a true story. A twelve-year-old girl asked her mother whether or not it was possible to become pregnant without being married. The mother, fearful of giving the girl "ideas," answered that it was not possible to get pregnant unless one had in fact gotten married. When this woman's older daughter learned of the answer her mother had given, she insisted that the mother talk to the girl again. The mother reluctantly did, and discovered to her horror that her little twelve-year-old daughter had been having intercourse with the boy down the street and was really inquiring whether or not she could get pregnant from these experiences. The mother, in believing that talking about sex equaled giving permission, narrowly escaped a family tragedy.

If we are reasonably confident about anything, it is this: the risk related to talking about sex and birth control with teenagers is far less than the risk associated with not talking about it. As we have noted, it's astonishing how many girls get pregnant because they have accepted what appears to be the parental message: If you talk or think about it, you'll do it; if you prepare for sex or you premeditate it, there's something wrong with you. The mass media only reinforce the message: "How romantic it is to just let it happen." Birth control is conspicuously absent from movies, television and romance novels. These matters are discussed in the better young-adult books, such as those by Judy Blume and Gloria D. Miklowitz, which provide an opportunity for some rehearsal on the adolescent's part.

> ► My twelve-year-old daughter wants to go to a boy-girl party, and I'm not convinced there are going to be any adults present.

Our response is not to let her go. If she is prepared to let you make some calls directly to the parents in whose home the party is to be held, that may be another matter. It's really a good idea for you and your spouse to come to some agreement about the age at which a child would be permitted to go to parties where no adults are present. Even more important, decisions have to be made about when it is okay to trust a child to go on a car date. Such conditions as meeting and becoming acquainted with the boy involved are essential. Again, we recognize that these are not simple matters; if the parents in the neighborhood could discuss these issues among themselves, life could be much easier.

This, of course, raises the issue of when parents should allow their youngsters to begin dating, one of the all-time best-selling questions among parents and an exceedingly difficult one to answer. Age itself is not the critical factor. Some children at thirteen and fourteen are more mature than others at seventeen and eighteen. The kind of questions you should ask yourself would be: How old is the date? Have you met him or her? Can you meet the date's parents or at least call them? Will a car be used? Where are the couple going? What time will they come home? Are you reachable by telephone if need be? And especially, what is your own comfort level with regard to the specific dating situation?

Beyond all that, it's a good idea to have open discussions among your neighbors, the local PTA and religious groups on what can reasonably be expected from children in your locality these days. We acknowledge being vague in our response to this subject, but frankly we prefer that both parents settle the issue on the basis of this kind of discussion rather than establish an arbitrary age rule which might not be appropriate for your situation.

> ► *It seems that a lot of parents worry that their children will begin dating too young, but our problem is just the opposite. Our son is now seventeen, and so far has shown almost no interest in girls. We've tried to encourage him to date, but he never responds, and just shrugs it off. Does this mean there's something wrong with him?*

Here again the issue is not that he doesn't want to date—quite a few normal young men are simply not ready for dating—but rather, what else may or may not be happening in his life? How is his performance in school? Does he have friends? Does he pursue constructive leisure-time interests? Is it possible that his disinterest in dating is rooted in a feeling of inferiority and a fear that nobody will like him—a terror of rejection? If you suspect other complications, don't deal directly with the obvious issue of dating, but rather concern yourself with the possible underlying reasons for his problems, such as low self-esteem. You may decide that counseling or therapy is the best way to help your son resolve his underlying problems.

> ► *My wife and I simply can't get used to the idea that our fifteen-year-old daughter is calling boys up on the phone, sometimes even asking them if they want to see a movie with her. Is this kind of aggressive behavior common these days?*

To tell you the truth, the mother of the boy probably isn't happy about this situation, either. Those of us who grew up in the days when girls were not supposed to be so "forward" are sometimes chagrined by their daughters' behavior. It gets labeled "aggressive" because taking the initiative has traditionally been a male prerogative. Yet a girl calling a boy these days is usually not so much aggressive as *assertive* behavior. Among adults, such behavior is becoming part of our culturally accepted norms, and adolescents tend to emulate what they observe in the older population. Things have changed; Sadie Hawkins Day used to be a once-a-year affair, but is now entering the mainstream of our daily lives.

Of course, it's possible for a girl to become openly aggressive in calling boys, making demands, even pushing for sexual relations with her boyfriend. This may disguise an underlying insecurity and a low self-esteem in girls who fear that if they don't make the move no boy will be interested in them. In these situations parents might do well to explore their daughter's feelings in an understanding, helpful way. Criticizing your daughter or insisting that she stop will not be helpful (even if the behavior itself stops).

There is, however, nothing wrong with establishing rules about when and for how long your daughter can stay on the phone, especially if the family has only one number, or if getting homework completed is a problem.

> ► *My sixteen-year-old son has been dating a girl for about six months, and lately they have been seeing much less of each other. I suspect that sexual tension and pressures between them are at the heart of it, but I'm not sure how or if I should broach the subject with my son.*

This is a fairly common situation which develops between adolescents. One of them (usually the boy) is pressuring the other to have sexual intercourse, or to have more sexual contacts than the other feels comfortable with. Young people are often not well-prepared to communicate about this problem between themselves, and the result is that the relationship goes downhill.

A concerned parent can make a neutral comment such as "I've noticed you haven't been seeing So-and-So lately—would you mind if I made some guesses as to the reason why?" and wait to see how the child responds. It's possible that the child won't want to discuss the issue, but chances are good that he or she can't talk to friends seriously about it and will welcome the opportunity for an adult viewpoint. Adolescents sometimes feel pressured to push for sex with a boyfriend or girlfriend, when they're more interested in the broader aspects of the relationship and doing fun things together. Parents can explore the child's feelings about it and express their own feelings on the matter (without excessive moralizing).

► *I suspect that my fifteen-year-old daughter and her boyfriend are becoming sexually involved (though I don't think they've had intercourse). I've walked into the den a couple of times while they've been in there and it always seems as if they're buttoning up and straightening out their clothes. Should I say anything?*

While we believe strongly that adolescents of your daughter's age shouldn't have sexual intercourse, it's not such a simple matter when discussing other forms of sexual expression. This seems to be a matter for individual families to work out for themselves in terms of acceptable values and behaviors. Some parents feel that hugging and kissing, petting and even mutual masturbation are acceptable forms of sexual discovery for adolescents. The problem is, parents worry that once their children start, they can't stop. Some parents, of course, don't want their children to engage in any sexually related activity. No matter what parents think about it, chances are their children will "make out."

We think you should talk to your daughter. However much we may have repeated this, we'd like to say again that talking about something is neither license, permission nor encouragement. In fact, our best review of all the research on this subject reveals that young people who are able to talk with their parents about these intimate details are more likely to delay their first sexual experiences, and when they do have intercourse, to use contraception.

This is not to suggest that you go into intimate detail about all the sexual things they've done already. It's much wiser to have a general discussion, and to give what constitutes your best judgment.

► *For the third time in his high-school career, our son is going steady with a girlfriend (he's sixteen, she's fifteen and a half). It worries us somewhat how intensely attached he seems to get to these girls, and how crestfallen he is when they separate. Is this something most teenagers go through these days? The situation is now even more com-*

plicated, as they want to go on a weekend camping trip with some other steady couples. Should we put our foot down?

Falling in and out of love is in fact a fairly common experience for young people. As we have suggested elsewhere, it's not a good idea to make fun of the youngster or in any way imply that it's part of his or her immaturity. Like everything else, your son's going steady should be seen in context. It's one thing if the love affair contributes to the self-esteem of the youngster and he or she is still doing schoolwork, paying attention to personal grooming and so forth. It's entirely another matter when the opposite occurs. It's really up to the parents to put the question into perspective and then decide how strict or trusting they want to be on related issues such as an overnight camping trip.

It seems perfectly legitimate to ask your son to hold off on that camping trip until a sense of trust and confidence has been established in the relationship between him and his steady girlfriend. You could say, "I'm not about to let you go on a trip as long as your schoolwork is in jeopardy," and so forth. The focus therefore is on the objective reality of the situation, rather than on whether or not you approve of his girlfriend or have some reservations about his going steady. The chances are that whatever you do will not be satisfactory to your son at this point. But that's where sticking to your best judgment counts.

► *My husband and I have just learned some very upsetting news. Our neighbor's son heard some boys talking about our sixteen-year-old daughter, and they were referring to her as a "slut" who'd put out for just about any boy who asked. We really love our daughter, and it really tears us up to think that she'd treat herself so badly. But we're afraid that if we say anything to her she'll feel we're accusing her. What if it isn't true?*

A lot of people think that the "sexual revolution" has eliminated the proverbial problem of a girl getting a "bad reputation," but this is not the case. Not only in small rural communities, but also in suburbs and cities, teenagers of both sexes circulate rumors (and occasional true stories) about who's willing to "do it." Parents need to be careful about how they handle any information, because sometimes "rumors" are started by insecure, boastful or vengeful boys, or by jealous, insecure girls, and have little or no basis in reality. On the other hand, some girls do behave promiscuously. (We use the word "promiscuous" to refer to a series of self-damaging sexual experiences usually devoid of intimacy for the individual.) Very often the sexual behavior is compulsive and indicates very low self-esteem on the girl's part (boys too, of course, can be promiscuous, but they don't seem to suffer as much as the girls do from bad reputations).

In a situation such as yours there seems to us to be no substitute for confronting the problem, not by yelling or blaming but by talking to your daughter, even at the risk of a bitter angry denial (or making a false assumption). You could say, "Look, you can't blame us for being worried. If it were your own daughter, wouldn't you?" Or another possibility would be, "Let's see what we can do about the false rumor," even to the point of volunteering to call the parents of the boy or boys involved.

► *For the last two months my son has been seeing a girl whom neither my husband nor I like. She seems to come from a decent family, but her clothes are usually dirty, she uses a lot of profanity and is rude to us, and treats our son pretty badly as well (he doesn't object, however). We've tried to talk to him about this, but he simply refuses to consider our ideas, and claims that we don't understand her or their relationship.*

The situation of children bringing home "undesirables" is so common that it's one of the things parents fear most. With all their grand hopes for their children, parents are horrified when their daughter waltzes in with Rasputin, or their son becomes enamored of the Wicked Witch of the West. Parents object to these boyfriends/girlfriends because they are of different religions, unemployed, from a lower socioeconomic background, from the "wrong" political party, apparently of lower intelligence, sloppy, rude, childish, alcoholic, too old, too young, pregnant, etc. We could go on—and the chances are that your evaluation is correct, from your point of view.

But your child doesn't see it that way or couldn't care less and, besides, is in love.

Where do you go from here? What are your rights? You have a right to:

- be enthusiastic or not;
- give your opinion or not;
- go along or fight it all the way;
- go to (and/or pay for) the wedding—or not;
- operate on the assumption that it won't last (your child will come to his or her senses).

Of course you have these rights even if you realize that you don't own your children and that they will make up their own minds no matter what.

But there are a few things to keep in mind. Your response could make a bad situation worse by:

- making the child more determined (young people have strong autonomy needs);
- creating a confrontational atmosphere which propels your son or daughter into an antagonistic stance (sometimes the child gets carried away by the anger, and you then become the enemy);
- focusing on your own reason for the opposition, whereas the *overriding* issue is whether it is a mature, loving relationship.

We have heard of too many cases where young adults have, in retrospect, felt that their parents were right: "If only I had listened to them. But I couldn't. They were so mean, so insensitive, I was determined to have my own way."

Obviously, there are just as many circumstances where parents have been wrong and lived to regret it. Some were able to patch things up; some were not.

What to do? First a few don'ts:

- Don't make it a test of wills.
- Don't start out by saying things like "How could you do this to me?," "After all I've done for you!," "When I was your age . . ."

- Don't break off relations.
- Don't say, "You'll get over it," "It's puppy love," "You can't be serious."

What to do?

Keep channels of communication open. It doesn't matter how angry or hostile you are. You must be civil to the person your child loves. Politeness is a good way of maintaining distance and leaves the situation open for review. If your child complains about your lack of enthusiasm, you say, "It isn't fair to force me to pretend, but he [or she] is welcome to our home."

Convey to your child that you know he or she will make up his/her own mind, and that you'll stand by him or her no matter what, but that you reserve the right to give your opinion.

Of course, if you are already in an antagonistic situation and have made some of the mistakes we've enumerated, it's going to be tough. But it may not be too late, especially if you acknowledge to your child that you were mistaken in your approach: "But, my dearest one, it is all right for us to disagree on some points, isn't it?"

Ask your child to concentrate on whether the relationship is a mature one. (See the section on mature and immature relationships in Chapter 9, "For Teenagers and Young Adults.")

HOMOSEXUALITY

▶ *My wife and I have been in a panic ever since our son announced to us last week that he is a homosexual. How can a seventeen-year-old boy know himself well enough to even know what he is? We feel as if we've just lost our son.*

It is all right to hope that one's children will not grow up to be homosexuals. Due to discrimination and hostility, the life of a homosexual can be very difficult. And, of course, parents and other family members often suffer, believing that they have done something "wrong" which has contributed to the situation.

Our advice is to be perfectly sympathetic—no jokes, no derisive comments such as "You must be kidding" or "You'll get over it." Don't rush your child to a physician or a psychiatrist for "straightening out." The best first response is, "I'm so glad you feel free to tell us [me] about this. Let's talk. How long have you felt this way? How do you feel about it?" The point is to encourage a full and open discussion.

The child should be encouraged to be open-minded and to make no final decision about the matter until adulthood. Try not to give the message that homosexuality is evil or sinful: simply convey that the teenager is too young to decide. In any case, reassure the child that if he or she has had fantasies or even a pleasurable experience with a member of the same sex, this is not sufficient grounds for a lifetime decision. Experimental homosexual behavior, such as mutual masturbation, is common during the early adolescent years (ages eleven to fourteen or so), especially among boys. It is rarely a precursor of homosexuality in later life, and for most boys it is simply a developmental phase of their sexuality.

Young people have declared themselves to be homosexual and have then been rejected by their families. The rejection has created enormous problems and has even resulted in many (especially males) becoming prostitutes.

Teenagers who "come out" typically encounter severe ostracism. Very few peer groups can tolerate this kind of acknowledgment. Yet some people would be greatly relieved if their sexual orientation were revealed. In some of the larger cities in this country gay and lesbian groups have provided clubs and recreational facilities for adolescents who want to identify themselves as homosexual. In general, these are few and far between and could serve only a small fraction of young people.

The following case study could be illuminating from a number of perspectives. An eighteen-year-old male student came to one of us and said, "I was one of your students. I need help. I have something terrible to confess. Can I trust you?" He received the following response: "No." He, in turn, responded, "What do you mean? You are supposed to be trusted." "I know, but I don't know you. I don't know if I can be helpful. You don't know me. Trust comes only at the end of a relationship. All meaningful exchanges between people involve risk." The student, getting the point, said, "Okay, I'll risk it. I'm a homosexual." The conversation continued as follows:

"Do you want to be a homosexual?"

"Of course not."

"Have you ever had a homosexual experience?"

"Of course not, what do you take me for?"

"I don't know yet. Have you ever had a heterosexual experience?"

"Of course not, I'm a homosexual. You're making fun of me."

"So far the diagnosis is asexual. Tell me your life history. You have five minutes."

As it turned out, he recalled having had homosexual fantasies at age twelve or thirteen. He didn't know that they were normal. He felt overwhelmed with guilt, and he feared being "queer." The more guilt, the more compelling and more obsessive the thoughts; it became a self-fulfilling prophecy. Upon entering college, he searched for his identity in the index of a psychiatric textbook. It didn't help, because he had never had a homosexual experience, so he consulted an advanced psychiatric textbook, where he found the concept of latent homosexuality. He was then fully self-diagnosed, without having had any sex experience.

Our view is that there is no such thing as a latent homosexual. You might as well say that all women are latently pregnant. A person who is afraid of being homosexual or afraid of homosexuals isn't necessarily homosexual. It could just mean that the person is afraid.

The above case history is important because there are many individuals who suffer from misinformation, teasing or downright harassment. Peers often cruelly accuse people of being queer or gay for reasons related to popular stereotypes. The so-called effeminate male or "butch" female—blatant types who flaunt their homosexuality, often to protest the hostility of the "straights"—probably constitute only 5 percent of the homosexuals in our society. It is terribly important to support people who are harassed or in any way threatened by a peer group.

Society will have to accept the idea that it is okay to be a homosexual. If a person feels that he or she is gay, yet, at the same time, wants to fight it ("to be cured"), the initial rejection of homosexual feelings uses up most of the energy needed to effect the change. In a sense, one needs to say, "If I am, I am, but if I could figure a way out of it, I'd prefer it." The parent may want to say to the child—or preferably think it—"I hope you aren't homosexual, but if you are, you remain my child. I will love you no less for it. I'm with you all the way." The part that must be verbalized is, "I'm with you all the way."

Despite all the research, no one really knows what the causes of homosexuality are. We deliberately state our position in this fashion because more and more research hasn't led to more and more understanding; in fact, it adds plausibility to the common-sense notion that the more we know, the less we know. We tend to be skeptical of researchers who "know."

Once upon a time, such researchers "knew" that if you had a weak father and a strong mother the chances of becoming a homosexual were pronounced. Most professionals in the field only recently discarded this theory. Apparently, researchers started out with the erroneous assumption that all homosexuals were in a state of arrested development. Lately, professionals have also taken another look at American families: it appears that many consist of strong mothers and weak fathers and most of them do not have homosexual children. In addition, virtually all the research on homosexuals has been done on patients in therapy. This would be analogous to concluding that hetero-sexuals are disturbed because more than 90 percent of people in therapy are heterosexual.

Only one thing is known with reasonable certainty: almost every homosexual was born to a heterosexual couple. The evidence of heredity, hormonal imbalance and interactional pat-terns of parents is very sparse and lacking credibility.

While cause remains a hotly debated issue, leading scholars have settled on the likelihood that a person's sexual orientation is pretty much determined by the age of four or five. Popular myths about the seduction and recruitment of children by ho-mosexuals are disputed by the established research in the field. Arguments against hiring homosexual teachers are similarly questioned. In any case, more than 90 percent of all child mo-lestation in schools involves heterosexual males and is directed at females. Should we bar heterosexual males from teaching in the public schools? Even if sexual identity were not determined by age five, it would be unrealistic to think that in a school where the teaching staff consists of 90 percent heterosexuals and 10 percent homosexuals, most of the children would flock to the latter. Are we eliminating heterosexuals as role models for children?

At one time professionals felt that people were *either* homosexual or heterosexual. Freud, however, postulated that all of us were born with a potential for bisexuality, capable of enjoying sexual experiences with either sex. Some writers in this field have even suggested that everyone would be bisexual if there were fewer social, moral and legal prohibitions against it. We don't subscribe to the either/or theory, and believe that the large majority of people are predominantly heterosexual, with perhaps 5 to 10 percent predominantly homosexual and 5 to 10 percent predominantly bisexual. Alfred Kinsey fairly well destroyed the either/or notion with his monumental research of the 1940s and 1950s. He suggested that people's sexual behavior could be categorized as follows:

0: Exclusively heterosexual behavior.
1: Largely heterosexual but incidental homosexual behavior.
2: Largely heterosexual but more than incidental homosexual behavior.
3: Equal amounts of heterosexual and homosexual behavior.
4: Largely homosexual but more than incidental heterosexual behavior.
5: Largely homosexual behavior but incidental heterosexual behavior.
6: Exclusively homosexual behavior.

Kinsey's studies suggested that about 4 percent of males and 2 percent of females were probably exclusively homosexual. By the time they reach middle age, about 50 percent of males and 29 percent of females have had an overt erotic experience with a member of their own sex. He further suggested that 37 percent of all males and 13 percent of females had at least one homosexual experience to the point of orgasm between adolescence and old age. The Institute for Sexual Research founded by Alfred Kinsey has defined a homosexual as an adult who has had more than six sexual experiences with members of his or her own gender. On that basis, it is estimated that people with a predominantly homosexual orientation constitute about 10 percent of the population of the United States (more males than females). It has generally been estimated that less than 10 percent of the homosexual population has "come out of the closet," that is, openly identified themselves as being gay.

Regarding rights and discrimination, we stand with the majority of well-informed people in the country who believe that people who happen to be homosexual are entitled to the same civil rights as heterosexuals. We strongly feel that any other position is simply bigotry.

We do not think that erotic desire and fantasy constitute the only elements in determining a person's sexuality. Our definition of a homosexual is, "A person who, in his or her *adult life*, has and prefers sexual relations with members of the same sex." A person could have many homosexual fantasies and experiences and still not be a homosexual. Recent Masters and Johnson studies reveal that even exclusive heterosexuals acknowledge having homosexual fantasies. The idea that thoughts and even some experiences make one a homosexual could have a devastating impact on a person's life.

A true story might provide an appropriate illustration. Two fourteen-year-old boys regularly went to the attic after selling newspapers. There they would masturbate each other while looking at "girlie" magazines. On one occasion one of the boys picked up a male-body-builder magazine and looked at it. The other boy immediately said, "What's the matter with you, are you a faggot?" The fear that the partner might be homosexual negated the pleasurable experience. This story, described to us by one of our students, illustrates how ludicrous thinking can be about the topic. Both boys grew up heterosexual. Neither has been known to have had any further homosexual interests or experiences.

Many parents do not have to deal with their child's homosexuality because most children simply do not confide in them. Some parents prefer not to know. There are those who know and prefer to pretend they don't. We've heard of families whose children informed their parents of their homosexual orientation only to find out that the family couldn't cope with this knowledge. They interpreted this revelation as a rejection of everything they stood for, sometimes to the point of disinheriting their children, both financially and emotionally.

We also know families who developed a new family solidarity when a son or a daughter revealed a homosexual orientation. Parents should accept that being taken into confidence is a sign of trust, and should recognize, too, that it is psychologically better for the child to be able to acknowledge his or her sexual orientation rather than suffer a nagging worry about being "found out." For concerned parents, we recommend reading *Consenting Adult*, Laura Hobson's sensitive novel based on her personal experience. Also, get in touch with the National Gay Task Force (80 Fifth Avenue, New York, NY 10011). This group can put you in touch with other parents of gay children who are willing to serve in a supporting capacity. Another organization to benefit parents of gays is PARENTS FLAG (Parents and Friends of Lesbians and Gays), which has established parent groups throughout the country.

It is important to realize that most homosexuals manage well. They are mature, healthy people who are contributing, responsible members of society. Although significant numbers are neurotic, this can be said about heterosexuals as well. Perhaps one day a person's sexual orientation will be of no concern to anyone and people will be judged solely by their character and actions. We also should keep in mind that homosexuality is not a lifestyle—it is a sex style. Homosexuals exist in all walks of life. They espouse the same range of political and philosophical positions as are found among heterosexuals.

Homosexuals are more visible these days, yet no evidence exists to suggest that there are, in fact, more homosexuals. The real change lies in the fact that they are more open to discussion, and generally more accepting of themselves.

► *Our thirteen-year-old son is very preoccupied with his male gym teacher. He is constantly talking about him, and it has reached the point where at least my husband is quite jealous. There are even times when my son tries to settle arguments based on his gym teacher's supposed opinion on the subject. We're not really concerned that our son is a homosexual, but we feel that his intense involvement may indicate some serious problems. He is also so involved in a sports training program that he shows no interest in having friends.*

We frequently encounter young adolescents having crushes on teachers of either sex, or engaging in hero worship (the idealization of movie stars or sports figures). While these are not uncommon incidents and may represent a perfectly normal and passing phase, they could be problematic. Your son's situation doesn't seem too serious, because from what is suggested by your question he is engaging in productive activities. There would be nothing wrong, however, in pointing out how he uses his admiration for the teacher as a weapon against his parents. There would also be nothing wrong in having a talk with the teacher directly, saying how much you appreciate his interest, and referring to some of your concerns. You should consider this especially if you suspect that the relationship between the teacher and your child is exploitative or otherwise not completely healthy; a situation of hero worship can be problematic if it blocks constructive interests. It is one thing to admire a movie or rock star, but if that preoccupation results in deterioration of schoolwork or is a substitute for developing friends, it is another matter entirely. The strategy should be not to attack the idol, but only the behavior about which you are concerned.

PORNOGRAPHY

▶ *My husband and I consider ourselves to be fairly open-minded, but when it comes to our children, it's much harder to be objective. While cleaning my son's room this afternoon (he's fourteen) I found some pornographic magazines in his closet. I wasn't snooping, and the magazines weren't even well-hidden. In a way it's funny, because I can remember reading anecdotes about mothers finding these things in their sons' rooms. But we're also worried—this wasn't just nudity, but real hardcore pornography (some of the photos displayed people getting into bondage and discipline—sadomasochistic acts). Are these things harmful?*

Some people feel that if they are to succeed in instilling in their children a sense of sexual integrity, they must keep them away from pornography at all costs. Pornography is held up as the enemy of healthy adjustment, in the ranks of drug abuse and criminal behavior.

We do not feel that pornography is appropriate for children (though we don't know how to stop them from seeing it). Most children at some point will encounter it or become interested for a time; even children with askable parents, from homes where sexuality has been openly discussed, may have their curiosity aroused by pornography.

Governments have often treated pornography as a social menace. This attitude has traditionally been based on the assumption that exposure to pornography has harmful effects on people. Furthermore, the legislatures of most Western countries have never been able to define it successfully. This task, for better or worse, has fallen to the courts.

Three basic theories exist to describe how pornography affects people. The first, or "modeling," theory argues that people imitate the sexual behavior that they witness in pornography. A second, or "cathartic," theory suggests that exposure to pornography *lessens* pent-up sexual drives, thus mitigating the possibility of antisocial or violent sexual behavior. The third, or "null," theory states that pornography has neither a stimulative nor a depressive effect on human sexual behavior.

Most contemporary research indicates that pornography is not harmful and does not corrupt. In this respect, the Danish experience is instructive. During the 1960s, Denmark experienced a rapid increase in the availability of pornography following its legalization. Sociological studies demonstrated that the overall number of sex crimes in Denmark *declined* in proportion to the *rising* availability of pornography. At this point it is premature to conclude that pornography lowered the number of sex crimes in Denmark. Other factors could be involved. Yet we can note that wide availability *did not* lead to an *increase* in any category of sexual offenses during the period under study.

Few psychiatrists believe that pornography causes individual pathology. Of the 3,423 psychiatrists who responded to a questionnaire on this subject, 80 percent reported *never* encountering an individual whose contact with pornography appeared to be a factor contributing to antisocial sexual behavior. Only 9 percent suspected such cases. About 7 percent were convinced they knew of such cases. Similar responses were received from professionals in child guidance, psychology and social work. For instance, 77 percent of these individuals responded "No" to the question "Do you think reading obscene books plays a significant role in causing juvenile delinquency?"

We do not think that pornography is educational; but there are at least two persuasive arguments against banning adult access to it. The first has to do with "forbidden fruit." The second involves the constitutional right of adults to look at or read anything they want to. (We endorse laws which make it illegal to distribute pornography to juveniles.) It is of interest to note that December 1982 marked the fiftieth anniversary of the publication of Erskine Caldwell's *Tobacco Road*. Widely banned and considered pornographic at the time, it is now hailed as a significant contribution to American literature.

Our view is that if you ban pornography, you allow criminal elements who already control most of its production and distribution to earn more money. Anything that's banned immediately becomes more expensive and often more readily available. The more governmental regulation and restriction, the more possibility of organized criminal activity and control. Society should have learned a lesson from Prohibition.

The energy consumed in banning pornography would be better spent in establishing good sex education in our schools. We should deal with the problems that cause the desire for pornography, instead of focusing on the symptoms. Most anti-pornography activity is simply headline-grabbing. People who are well sex-educated and well adjusted find pornography to be of little interest after a while. In fact, we think that a personal fixation on pornography is a symptom of emotional distress. We are not talking about readers of such magazines as *Playboy* or *Playgirl*. We mean pornography that degrades women and misuses children. Pornography does not belong on billboards or television. The violence and rape featured on TV, in our view, is the *grossest form of pornography.*

Here is an excerpt from a report by Sweden's State Commission on Aspects of Sex and Personal Relationships in Teaching and Public Education:

> Teaching should systematically combat the picture of the relationship between man and woman promulgated by pornography and "sexism." The separation of sexuality and sexual life from the context of life at large, and, particularly, the presentation of women purely as a sexual object, are incompatible with the objectives proposed for sexual education.

Pornography is a symptom of society's unwillingness to promote responsible sexuality education at home and in the schools.

Now to return to the question of what (if anything) to say to your son. Without knowing your son it's hard to predict his reaction were you to confront him with the "evidence," but it's a good guess that he might be embarrassed, guilty, angry, defensive, apologetic, frightened. Of course, he might have a healthy attitude about it, shrug it off and inquire whether you have a hang-up. You and your husband might want to be alert to his possible sources for obtaining the materials; unless your son looks eighteen, few adult-bookstore proprietors would admit him. This would imply that some older person was obtaining the materials for your son or his peers.

When talking with your son, an opening line to the effect "We realize that we're asking you to discuss a very private aspect of your life, but we've become concerned that you seem to be collecting pornography" might help to alleviate some of the anxiety surrounding the conversation. Leave your son room to *not* discuss his feelings, and be sure not to attack him or accuse him of anything—you are asking because you care deeply about his well-being. (Incidentally, it might be wise for just one parent to broach this subject; two parents might be construed as an interrogation.)

Above all, be cautious lest you give your son the impression that he is "sick," and don't suggest that he should see a psychotherapist (an alternative only when you suspect that a young person is fixated—i.e., that his involvement with pornography is becoming compulsive). For the majority of adolescents who develop an interest in pornography, it is a passing involvement;

hence, the suggestion that their curiosity is abnormal and "dirty" can do damage to their growing sense of identity. We prescribe patience for the parents—especially if, in other areas of his life, your son appears to be reasonably well adjusted.

LUST AND THE CONTEMPORARY RELIGIOUS DILEMMA

▶ *My wife and I are conservative Christians, and we find it exceedingly difficult to tolerate what we feel are your permissive attitudes toward lust. We believe that they violate the religious principles we've tried to pass along to our children. We have a fifteen-year-old son, and we don't want him to act on all of his lustful feelings.*

Lust in men appears to be a near-universal phenomenon, and in our society the prohibitions against it derive from Christ's pronouncement in Matthew 5:28: "But I say to you that every one who looks at a woman lustfully has already committed adultery with her in his heart." His message would seem to be clear, but contemporary theologians are now making a concerted effort to distinguish between *lust* and *fantasy*, two terms which have (erroneously) been used interchangeably.

A man who *lusts* after a woman (or another man) is pursuing a fantasy in an aggressive way; he meets her, his eyes scan her body, and he begins scheming ways to effect the seduction. His desire is his motivation. This is worlds apart from a developing relationship wherein sexual desire evolves in the context of the relationship itself. A man who *fantasizes* sexually about another person creates mental images in his mind and builds upon the scenario as he wishes. There is often little control over the appearance or disappearance of the thought itself, which may or may not be pleasurable to the individual. Day and night dreams which impinge upon us may involve being raped, ravaged, or witnessing one's own funeral, or they may be surreal and disconnected messages with no definite theme. The thoughts may be primitive symbols of the unconscious mind or may represent personal interest in a particular sexual situation. But they do not in themselves imply antisocial or sexist behavior, nor do they mean that the individual intends to live them out in real life. The theory that all dreams represent our real wishes is simply absurd. If a man accepts the fantasies as a healthy part of his personality, he will not suffer the obsessive repetition of the thoughts that are caused by guilt. For most men, the experience of both lust and fantasy can have physical as well as psychological ramifications. The stirring in the loins, the quickening pulse and other physiological responses accompany the mental process. That doesn't matter. What matters is the behavior which results.

If anything, Christ was saying that lust is a distortion of man's instinctual sexual drive. It is impersonal, a burden for women who resent being the objects of men's desire, and can become a hypnotic force to the man preoccupied with it. Writing in his book *Embodiment*, James B. Nelson states: ". . . if lust is untamed, inordinate sexual desire which is not only the passion for *possession* of another but which also becomes, by its centrality in the self, an expression of *idolatry*, then we are dealing here with something different from the usual erotic awareness expressed in sexual fantasy."

We would encourage you to view your son's behaviors and attitudes using these guidelines which, while maintaining respect and dignity for other human beings, do not seek to punish people for their sexual impulses alone. The book *Sex for Christians*, by Lewis B. Smedes, states: "Sensuous and sensual pleasure is good, and our desire for it is certainly not a distortion . . . Sensualism becomes a distortion of sexuality when it cuts physical pleasure in sex off from a personal quest for higher values. It distorts sexuality into a lust for physical pleasure that dominates one's sexual life."

CHAPTER NINE

For Teenagers and Young Adults (and Their Parents)

These are questions we have been asked many times by young people over the past twenty-five years. You may find that reading them will prepare you for questions your younger brothers and sisters or other relatives might ask. At times you may be helpful to your less-informed friends as well. Some teenagers are more askable than their parents.

Would it surprise you to learn that the most frequently asked question among young people is:

► *How can you tell if you're really in love?*

Why do so many people feel insecure about love? Why do people fall in and out of it? Why do we hear so many complaints regarding regrets and mistakes about love? Why is it, too, that if you are a teenager, adults (often parents) are quick to say, "It's puppy love," "You'll get over it," "Wait until you are older"? Can you fall in love more than once? Is love at first sight worth much—or is it the best kind? Is it true that love is blind? Our response is that if love is blind, it had better not remain so for more than twenty-four hours. After that, open your eyes and see the person in a clear light.

If you feel yourself to be in love, you are. We're now referring only to the love for a special person, not for your parents, God or a popular hero. We suspect that one can love many people but can be *in love* with only one person at a time.

Lots of people wonder how they can tell if they're really in love. Are there any signs? The answer is yes, but first you need to know that there are two kinds of love. We might think of them as *mature* and *immature* love. It's not that difficult to know whether love is mature or immature. Immature love is exhausting. You see people going around declaring, "I'm in love! I'm in love! I'm in love!" It's even exhausting watching them. They don't have time to shower, do their schoolwork or help with household tasks. "How can I do the dishes? I'm in love!" Immature lovers often have what we call a hostile-dependent relationship. That means they don't enjoy being with those they supposedly love, yet they can't stand to be without them. When they're not with their partners, they miss them. But when they're together, they fight, argue and act in a jealous manner.

What do you do when the person you love is always asking, "Do you love me? Do you love me?" Say no, explain why you said that and you'll have your first genuine conversation.

When you are really in love you enjoy it. Mature love is energizing. You have enough time and energy for most of the things you want to do. When you are with your loved one you feel happy, joyous and secure. That doesn't mean you never fight. But most of the time you really want to please the other person. Your caring about the other person seems just a little more important than that person's caring for you.

People still ask, "How can I tell if I'm really in love? What happens?" Some people actually think that they'll be hit by a thunderbolt. They wait their whole lives for this to happen. They go through many relationships looking for a "dream" person, that perfect someone who will live up to their fantasies. They don't realize that there is no such person.

Mature love is a slowly developing, exciting experience. Many relationships don't start out that way, but with effort and time they can become mature. The relationship does need to be mature before you settle down and take on shared responsibilities such as marriage and children.

Mature love is not motivated by a desire to be taken care of.

If you feel that you are nobody unless somebody loves you, you'll be nobody after somebody loves you. No one can validate who you are. You need to feel good about yourself in order to be good to anybody else.

If you are really in love, you allow yourself to open up to the other person. Moving toward intimacy in this way involves a *risk*: risk that the other person will still love you, risk that you won't be rejected. You also allow for mistakes, troubles and periods of unhappiness. Many people think that sex is the most important part of love. This is not true. Caring deeply for another person is something quite apart from being turned on by a part of the body like a breast, a bicep or a rear end.

If people can love each other in a mature way, they can make choices. They will marry for love.

How can you tell if you're really in love? You can tell by the energy you have.

▶ *What can I do if nobody likes me?*

Maybe you believe that other people are responsible for your feelings, that others *make* you feel upset, hurt, angry or happy. But, with the exception of physical pain, you make yourself feel just about every emotion you experience. Your way of thinking causes your emotions.

Self-acceptance has little to do with what other people think of you. With self-acceptance, you define yourself as worthy of existing. You just are. You are not the same as your behavior. Accept yourself and strive to change your behavior so that it expresses your best self.

Remember that each of us is a fallible human being. All human beings make mistakes. If you are able to apply this idea not only to yourself, but also to others, you will not need to engage in self-blame (guilt or anxiety) or other-blame (hostility).

People who are self-accepting are attractive to some other people. People who have poor self-esteem and express it in being (not looking) unattractive tend to repel rather than attract others.

If you feel depressed, the best way to get out of it is to do something productive or learn something new. Another way is to be helpful to those less fortunate than yourself. You'll feel yourself likable when you have a vision of life as an opportunity rather than a burden. You will be more attractive!

▶ *Is it all right for teenagers to have sex?*

We don't think so. The risks are too great. More than one million teenage girls get pregnant each year. About the same number contract STD (sexually transmitted disease, sometimes called venereal disease, or VD). Each year many thousands of teenagers spoil their whole lives by having babies at age thirteen, fourteen or fifteen or by becoming sterile (losing their capacity to have or father babies) because of untreated STD.

We really mean *spoil* because so many teenagers drop out of school as a result of pregnancy and lose their opportunities to get good jobs, be self-supporting and even get married and have a decent family life. Teenage girls fall rather easily for lines like "If you really love me you'll have sex with me." Afterward, they are abandoned.

Adolescence is a time for excitement, boy-girl get-togethers and testing out relationships. Why spoil these opportunities to figure out what you want and need with a heavy sexual trip that almost no young person can handle? Sex is never a test of love. Only a period of caring, of developing a trusting relationship, can reveal the true nature of love.

It is difficult to imagine that any teenager—mature or otherwise—can handle the consequences of a pregnancy or the pain of developing a reputation for being "easy." We realize that teenagers are under a lot of pressure to conform, but don't kid yourself. Most teenagers under seventeen have not had sexual relations, and those who have had sex find it, for the most part, a pretty disappointing experience. They didn't realize that the first experience of sex, especially for adolescents, is usually grim. Very seldom is it enjoyable, even though most young people won't admit it.

We feel it's better to wait until you are older. Older means at least eighteen, when you are away at college or working outside the home. At that age, young people have relatively easy access to birth-control methods and have had some experience with relationships. They can make some judgments about their readiness for sexual intercourse. They should know that it's even all right to wait until marriage.

Many young people find that they can be sexual with each other without having intercourse. A lot of young couples have discovered that they can be very sexual and loving with each other by hugging, kissing and caressing.

We know what is often said: "Once you start, you can't stop." That's a lot of baloney. It's a line used mostly by boys for their own purposes. If a boy reaches his "peak of passion" and says he can't stop, all you have to say is, "I hear someone coming" (no pun intended). He'll stop on a dime. We do know that some young people will have sex whether we like it or not and whether their parents like it or not. We advise them at least to use a reliable method of birth control. It is wrong to bring an unwanted child into this world. It's not romantic to have sex without birth control, nor is it spontaneous. It's just plain stupid.

Of course, we know that there are some teenagers at sixteen or seventeen who have mature love affairs. Some of these young people are more mature than some adults. We still think they ought to wait. Maybe it seems unfair, but it is better to wait and "suffer a little" than to be sorry for a lifetime.

▶ *How can you tell if someone is handing you a line?*

If someone says, "If you really love me, you'll have sex with me," it's *always* a line. If that someone threatens to leave you if you don't (it's usually the boy telling the girl, but not always), then that person doesn't really care about you anyway.

Until such time as boys and girls stop playing games with each other, one should be prepared to play games in order to protect oneself. Here are some common lines with suggested answers:

HE: Let's go upstairs. I'd like to check your vault and perhaps make a deposit.

SHE: Your credit is no good. Take me home.

HE: Where have you been all my life?

SHE: Not waiting around for you.

SHE: Where have you been hiding?

HE: From you, my dear.

SHE: Would you like me to seduce you?

HE: When I'm ready, I'll let you know.

HE: Would you like to get in the back seat of the car?

SHE: I prefer to sit up front with you.

HE: If we don't have sex, I'll go crazy.

SHE: Go.

HE: If you don't stay over, you'll never know what you're missing.

SHE: Yes, I know already.

HE: How can you do this to me?

SHE: You are doing it to yourself.

HE: You don't love me.

SHE: You are forcing me to have some second thoughts about it.

HE: Don't worry, I'll use protection.

SHE: You'll need protection if you don't leave me alone.

Here are some good ways of saying no:

- That's a line.
- No.
- I don't feel like it.
- No, it's against my religion.
- I have a headache.
- I don't know you well enough.

Finally, here is the ultimate line:

HE: I just oiled my machine. Want to see how it works?

SHE: (The ultimate put-down) Why don't you give it a cold shower and see if it rusts?

One day, people will realize that getting to know each other is truly the bottom line.*

▶ *Do guys really respect you more if you say no?*

It would be easy for us to say, "Of course they do," and we'd be sure that you wouldn't believe us. The fact is that some do, and some don't. We feel very strongly that those who don't, care more about sex than they do about you. In many respects a good test of how much a male cares about you is his willingness to continue seeing you even if you don't have sex with him. What's really sad is when a girl feels that her only attraction is her sex appeal. Instead of promoting self-esteem, this leads to one exploitative situation after another. When boys are pre-occupied with sex appeal instead of a relationship with a girl, they are invariably disappointed and look for somebody else who's closer to their fantasy. The dynamics here are usually that the boy feels inferior and is looking for a sex object to enhance his own self-esteem.

When you get right down to it, there's no substitute for a good friendship which might develop into a close love relationship.

► *How can you distinguish between possessiveness and love?*

Love is when you enjoy, respect and appreciate another person. Possessiveness is when you try to control and dominate another person. Excessive jealousy and anger are the chief signs of possessiveness.

► *I'm thinking about getting married. How can I be sure if it's the right thing to do?*

Don't if:

- when you are together, you spend most of your time disagreeing and quarreling.
- one of you is relentlessly asking, "Do you love me? Do you really love me?"
- you get bored spending a day together without watching TV.
- you feel he or she has traits you can't stand.
- he or she makes promises—like "Don't worry, when we get married I'll stop drinking [or stop fooling around]." If it's something you absolutely don't approve, the person must make good on commitments before marriage. A bad situation usually gets worse after marriage.
- your prospective mate insists that you drop all your old friends and start a whole new social life.
- you are getting married only to escape a bad home situation.
- you are under twenty years of age.

- you don't get along with one of your parents, and your prospective mate seems "just like" that troublesome parent.
- you've done some soul searching and discover you're marrying a "sex object."
- you disagree on whether or not to have children.
- you are being influenced mainly by the flattery or wealth of the in-laws-to-be.
- you don't agree on a basic lifestyle. Is it going to be a marriage of equals, or a traditional marriage with the man as the "president" and the woman as "vice-president"?
- you are of different religions and you can't agree on how the children should be raised.
- you don't plan to give your marriage priority over all else.

► *Is it still considered normal to wait until marriage to have sex even though everyone else seems to have had sex already?*

Yes, it's normal. No one should feel compelled to have sexual experiences before he or she is ready. It doesn't matter whether readiness is influenced by moral or religious reasons or simply by emotional maturity. A lot of people are intimidated by peer group pressure to have sex and often find themselves exploited by the experience and humiliated that they didn't stick to their own values.

On the other hand, no one should have unrealistic expectations about waiting until marriage and assume that on the wedding night the couple will be rewarded by having mutual orgasms. Most initial sexual experiences are not that exciting. In general, we need to understand that sexual compatibility is a learned process.

► *Can you tell if a girl is a virgin?*

A virgin is a person who has not had sexual intercourse.

The hymen, made of skin tissue, partially blocks the entrance to the vagina of many females who haven't had sexual intercourse. In quite a large number of females the hymen is ruptured due to exercise, masturbation or for reasons that are not known. Often one cannot tell if a female is a virgin unless she is willing to tell you.

The first experience(s) of sexual intercourse can be painful for women. Sometimes, but not always, there can be some bleeding. Gentleness in initial insertion is important.

Some boys who boast about having many partners say that when they marry they will marry virgins. Our response is we hope you'll marry a person, not a hymen. Only men who are themselves virgins are entitled to expect the same of their brides.

► *My girlfriend and I have been dating for four years. She is the only sexual partner I have had. Do you think I should have sex with someone else before I get married to her?*

What would be the point of having sex with someone else? The opportunities for variety are endless, even with one person. Why risk spoiling the relationship?

► *Is it all right for females to be assertive?*

Assertiveness is a good quality. It means that you know what your goals are and you strive to obtain them. It means learning how to stand up for your rights even in uncomfortable situations. (Assertiveness is different from being aggressive. Aggressiveness is being insensitive to the rights of others.)

A good exercise suggested by our colleague Oralee Wachter is to develop Your Own Bill of Rights.*

Here are some suggestions:

I have a right to   change my mind;
say I don't feel like it;
be responsible for my own sexual feelings;
ask for what I want;
enjoy hugging and kissing without it
meaning that I want sex;
not act macho;
refuse a date without feeling guilty;
say no;
say yes.

What are some rights you would like to add?

* This is but one of several exercises accompanying a remarkable film series entitled *Acquaintance Rape*, designed for high schools to deal with problems of rape among people who know each other. "Acquaintance Rape Prevention" is a multimedia package of four 16mm. films, teachers' guides, posters and role-playing cards. For use with coed audiences only. Available from O.D.N. Productions, Inc., 74 Varick St., New York, NY 10013.

I have a right to   1.
                        2.
                        3.
                        4.
                        5.
                        6.
                        7.
                        8.

► *Do men enjoy and/or appreciate initiation of sexual friendships by women?*
Many men do these days.

NORMAL / ABNORMAL

► *Is there a way of telling what is normal or abnormal sex between two people?*
Generally speaking, normal behavior is voluntary (both people consent to it). This behavior is not exploitative. It is free of guilt and serves to enrich the relationship. Abnormal behavior tends to be driven or compulsive. It has a tendency to hurt another person. It is usually selfish and exploitative.

► *Why do people have sex hang-ups in the first place?*
Hang-ups are cultural, passed from parents to children and picked up from society. If you aren't hung up about sex, chances are your children won't be.

► *What about your thoughts?*
What you do counts, not what you *think*. All thoughts are normal, no matter how weird. Difficulty arises if you feel guilty about a thought. Then you'll keep having it. Guilt is the energy for the repetition of unacceptable thoughts.

► *Are sexual fantasies normal during intercourse?*
Sexual fantasies are not only normal but common, and for some people they provide an added zest to the experience.

► *Why is it easier for males to have intercourse without emotional involvement than it is for most females?*
Contrary to popular belief, it is just as enjoyable for men to

have emotional involvements as for women. Unfortunately, there are still too many men who are responsive to the double standard and the expectations of the sexist society in which we live. They don't seem to be happier for it. With the growing impact of the women's-liberation movement this kind of question will ideally become obsolete.

▶ *Why is it that men and women always seem to get involved in power struggles over sex? It seems that men are always trying to have sex more often than their partner wants it.*

The joke you'll hear most often about this situation goes something like "Not tonight, dear—I have a headache." It's been suggested that such apparent differences in sex drives are due mainly to biological (hormonal) forces, and that they thus represent "natural" variations between the sexes. We don't agree with this point of view.

We believe that sexual desire is primarily a psychological phenomenon. In our society, men are programmed to feel they need sex; to men, intimacy, closeness and touching are equated with sexual intercourse. Thus, when a woman expresses a desire for closeness, the male often assumes that this means she wants intercourse (when what she really might want is to cuddle). And so at times it does appear as if a power struggle exists, in large part because there is often little or no communication between the partners about their desires.

Women's programming also plays a role in the conflict. Women tend to be raised to believe that sex is dangerous, and that "men are after only one thing." Thus they might tend to resist sex without knowing why (just as men might pursue sex without really feeling like it—what they really want might be cuddling or a massage).

▶ *I'm an eighteen-year-old girl and I've never reached an orgasm. Am I normal?*

Whether you have orgasms or not has little or nothing to do with being normal. What you need to know is that very few teenage women achieve orgasm the first times they have sex. Many will even acknowledge that sex isn't that great in its initial stages. Good sex has to do with shared intimacies, practice and feeling loved. Many women reach their first orgasm through masturbation, and some through mutual masturbation.

▶ *Is it true that "normal" people need sex every two or three days? Is it normal in a loving relationship to be satisfied with sex once a week?*

There is no such thing as a normal rate of sexual intercourse. Some enjoy it frequently and others infrequently. What counts is what's mutually satisfying. Of course you can have a satisfactory relationship having sex once a week.

▶ *Does the size of one's penis make a difference?*

No. Besides, you can't tell the size of an erect penis from observing its nonerect state. A lot of males worry because their penis seems small when compared with others'. What they don't know is that in an erect state their penis could be larger than those that appear huge in a nonerect state. A girl doesn't need to be concerned that a particular penis is too large for her. The vagina adjusts to any size penis.

▶ *Can you still be normal sexually if you have an aversion to oral or anal sex?*

People should be free to have any kind of sexual preference. There may be some problems if a person finds this experience revolting or disgusting. On the other hand, many people have perfectly normal, healthy sexual experiences without either oral or anal sex. They are, however, increasingly becoming part of the repertoire of sexually compatible couples.

▶ *What would you think about a person who doesn't seem to need sex at all? I'm a male senior, I've never had sex, I don't masturbate. I'm happy, I'm successful, but sex of any kind does not interest me personally. Do you think I'm normal?*

There is not necessarily anything wrong with someone who feels the way you do. Just as in the same way there's nothing wrong with anybody who decides to be celibate for the rest of his or her life, as is required in some religious orders. In any case, you can always change your mind and enter into sexual relationships at a later stage in your life—if that's what you'll want at the time. If, however, you are not happy about your low sex drive, or you suspect that there is some physical cause, you may want to seek professional guidance.

▶ *What about masturbation?*

It is normal and healthy for both males and females. No physical harm results even if you think you are doing it too much. Males don't have to worry that they will run out of sperm; a fresh supply is readily available. You need be concerned only if you seem to masturbate compulsively—that is, if you "can't help yourself" and don't enjoy the experience. Guilt is usually the energy behind compulsive masturbation.

SEXUAL RELATIONSHIPS

▶ *Do males and females have cycles during which they feel more sexual than at other times?*

We think sex has larger psychological components than physiological ones. Your relative state of sexual desire depends more on your mood and state of mind than on physical or hormonal cycles.

▶ *How can a sexual dialogue be started with a man so that he will respond to my individual needs?*

Try something like this: "Can I tell you some things about my sexual feelings which you could not possibly know about unless I told you?" His response will be, "Sure." Then lay it on him (but without being critical).

▶ *How can a girl tell if she has an orgasm?*

Orgasm is most often associated with pleasurable sensations related to the clitoris. But women can achieve orgasm from a wide range of sexual stimulations. A good way to think about orgasm is as a peak experience, intensely pleasurable, and then a nice relaxed feeling afterward. Women who have not experienced orgasms are often encouraged to masturbate as a good way to learn how.

▶ *Is it possible for a woman to achieve orgasm without the clitoris being stimulated?*

Yes.

▶ *I find direct clitoral stimulation painful.*
Some women do. Many women prefer indirect stimulation.

▶ *Is there a difference between ejaculation and orgasm in the male?*
Yes; ejaculation can occur without orgasm. Orgasm, however, is usually accompanied by ejaculation in males. This is not generally acknowledged, but men realize that there is a big difference in the intensity of orgasm at different times.

▶ *What is the best way to prevent ejaculation from happening immediately after entering the vagina?*
It is not unusual, during the first few times a man has sex or when circumstances are anxiety-filled, to have a premature ejaculation. If the problem is not solved soon enough for you, it could be due to fear of failure. A couple should then experiment with being together sexually for a few weeks without having sexual intercourse. Get to feel comfortable with each other without the need to "perform." Another approach which works with some males is to masturbate an hour or so before having sexual intercourse; some males last longer the second time around.

In any case, if the premature ejaculation persists, a sex counselor should be consulted, or, if you prefer, first read one of the books recommended for men in the bibliography to see if the advice and the exercises work for you.

▶ *When I have sex and come it takes me a long time, perhaps half an hour, before I can get hard again. Does that mean there is something wrong with me?*
No. It's called the refractory period. It takes a while for males to achieve an erection after ejaculating.

▶ *How can you persuade your partner to participate in oral sex?*
The best you can do is try to encourage your partner by suggesting that if he or she does not enjoy it you would not apply any more pressure. It does happen to be true that there are perfectly normal people who don't enjoy oral sex.

▶ *Do pot, alcohol or other drugs act as a sexual stimulant?*
Communicating with another person is a much better way to

heighten sexuality. Drugs may result in an artificial stimulation of certain senses, but they also tend to turn you in on yourself, thus cutting off the other person. Drugs tend to rob the experience of meaning. Furthermore, more than just a little alcohol tends to inhibit sexual responsiveness.

HOMOSEXUALITY

► *How can you tell if a person is homosexual?*

You can't unless they tell you. People simply are what they are. No one chooses to be a homosexual. Therefore, it is not okay to be antigay. This is true in the same respect that it is not okay to be anti–people who are left-handed.

A lot of young people worry about their own impulses. Many have homosexual thoughts or even a few experiences. This does not make them homosexual. A homosexual is a person who as an adult prefers relations with members of the same sex.

A young person might be approached by an adult homosexual—but much more often by an adult heterosexual—for the wrong reasons. The response should be, "No, thank you." Just walk away. The vast majority of homosexuals are just like the majority of heterosexuals. They do not try to seduce young people. Furthermore, they are pretty discreet about their own sexual behavior. That's why you can't tell whether or not a person is a homosexual just by observing behavior. Only a small number (about 10 percent) are deliberately effeminate (or masculine in the case of lesbians) and put on a "show," mainly to annoy people in a society that discriminates against homosexuals.

► *What causes a person to be homosexual?*

The causes of homosexuality remain unknown. Evidence suggests that people's sexual orientation is determined by the time they are five years old. Sexuality, whether it is heterosexual or homosexual, can be considered abnormal only if it is exploitative or self-destructive.

► *A friend of mine recently announced that he is a homosexual, and I'm having trouble deciding if I can remain friends with him.*

This is a fairly common situation, and one which sometimes

threatens people. Sometimes, the person to whom the news is revealed fears that the gay person will make a sexual overture. Although this is sometimes the case, usually the gay person divulged this personal information because he or she had grown uncomfortable with the secrecy, pretense and inauthenticity of hiding the true identity.

For years we have been conducting a survey among college students. One of the questions, along with possible responses, reads as follows:

> You discover that your best friend is homosexual when he/she reveals that he/she would like to have a sexual experience with you. What is your response likely to be?
>
> 1. One of distress. I would want to terminate the relationship.
> 2. I would refuse the invitation and say that our friendship depended on the homosexuality being kept private so that I wouldn't be subject to embarrassment.
> 3. I would refuse the invitation, but say that his/her homosexuality would not affect our friendship.
> 4. I might consider experimenting once with such an invitation, even though I'm pretty sure I'm heterosexual.
> 5. I would be pleased.

Of the 420 students responding to the most recent survey (fall 1982), 17.6 percent gave number 1 as their answer; 12.6 percent responded with number 2; 58.7 percent with number 3; 6.9 percent with number 4; 1.1 percent with number 5; and 3.1 percent gave no response at all. Over the past eight years, involving more than 7,000 students, the percentage of individuals giving a number 3 response has increased slightly each year from a base response of 45 percent.

Despite significant improvements in the last decade, popular polls and recent municipal elections suggest that a large number of Americans do not approve of gay rights. One need recall that our Constitution was designed to protect the basic rights of a minority, even if a majority does not approve. If our black population had to wait for a majority of people in the country to accept "equality of all before the law," we would still be where we were before the landmark Civil Rights Act of the recent past.

It is all right to have your personal opinion about homosexuality. It's not acceptable to harass or to discriminate just because you are in a position to do so. What consenting adults do in private is no one's business. There is something wrong with people who intrude into other people's private affairs. The people for whom we have the least respect are those who use the Bible to justify their hatred or bigotry. God's message to all of us is to "love thy neighbor as thyself."

> ► *As a female, I am constantly intrigued (turned on) by the female body, including my own. However, I don't relate this to my sexual preference. In fact, it increases my sexual desire for a man (I think). Is this possible? Or does this type of arousal indicate homosexual orientation?*

This is such a common feeling, but very few boys or girls are willing to acknowledge it to anyone else. Why shouldn't a body be a turn-on? It does not reveal a homosexual orientation. We're not suggesting that turn-ons represent an invitation to exploitation or are substitutes for relationships. It could just be a nice feeling. Homosexuality refers to a desire to have sexual relations only with members of the same sex.

CONTRACEPTION, PREGNANCY, STDs

> ► *Is the pill harmful?*

As of late 1982, the pill is still reported safe if taken under the direction of a doctor; in fact, it is safer than childbirth. Women with histories of diabetes, heart disease, liver malfunction, migraine headaches, high blood pressure or cancer should not be on the pill. Check with your doctor. Some women's groups are opposed to the pill. As a consequence of this influence more and more women are using the diaphragm.

> ► *What's the best method of birth control for people who are just starting out to have sex?*

The best protection would be to have both the male use a condom and the female use contraceptive foam. Neither requires a prescription. Both are available from most drugstores. Follow the directions on the labels. Both are necessary for protection against STD, as well as against unwanted pregnancy.

► *Are there any new methods of birth control coming out for men?*

Yes, but a pill for men is still in the future. The condom and a vasectomy (sterilization) are still the only two choices.

► *What effect does having a vasectomy have on your sex life?*

Vasectomy is a procedure to prevent the release of sperm when the male ejaculates. It is a simple operation which is done on an outpatient basis and has no ill effect on the sex life. As a matter of fact, many males report that their sex lives improve because there is no fear of impregnating their partner.

► *Is there any "safe" way or time to have sex without practicing birth control?*

Don't believe stories that you can't get pregnant if you have sex standing up, or if it's the first time, or if you've taken one pill, or if he pulled out in time. Withdrawal is not a good method because a few drops of semen are released from the penis before ejaculation, and these few drops contain sperm that can impregnate. Anytime you have unprotected sexual intercourse you risk pregnancy. Even though the risk is less a day or two before, during and after the period, there is still a risk.

► *Is it safe for a pregnant woman to have intercourse?*

Generally speaking, it is safe for pregnant women to have intercourse. Some women find that they don't feel like having sex during this time, while others find that pregnancy heightens their sexual desires. Men should be sensitive to these feelings.

Some new evidence, however, suggests that some women should avoid intercourse during the last trimester (three months) of pregnancy. This is especially the case for women with a history of miscarriages or with premature ripening of the cervix, something your doctor can diagnose. Recent, but not definitive, medical studies also suggest that *all* women should avoid intercourse in the last month of pregnancy because of a slight chance of triggering an early labor. An obstetrician would be able to advise each woman of what is best for her.

► *Is it possible to become pregnant without intercourse—that is, from sperm ejaculated right outside the vagina?*

Yes, but it is rare. It is also very rare for a girl to get pregnant from sperm on a guy's fingers.

▶ *How does rhythm work? What are the safest days for having intercourse?*

The safest days for having intercourse are a couple of days before a female's menstrual period, during the period itself and a couple of days after. Ovulation occurs about fourteen days before the onset of the next period; due to irregularities in women's cycles, this is impossible to predict with absolute certainty. It is now believed that every time a woman has unprotected intercourse she risks pregnancy. One way to become a parent is to rely on the rhythm method.

However, much scientific work is being done in this area of "natural" family planning; perhaps a reliable natural method of birth control will someday be available.

▶ *How many weeks after conception is it still relatively safe to have an abortion?*

The earlier you have an abortion, the safer. It is best to stay within the law—before twenty-four weeks. An early abortion, within the first twelve weeks after conception, carries less physical risk than childbirth and is less traumatic for the woman than a later abortion. It is now becoming apparent that, for a large majority of women, the psychological repercussions of an abortion are also less than those of an unwanted birth.

▶ *Is it safe for a woman to have more than one abortion?*

Generally speaking, it is safe—much safer than childbirth—for a woman to have one or two abortions. There is now some evidence, however, that multiple abortions—four or five or more—can jeopardize a woman's future chances of carrying a baby to term. Abortion should never be used as a form of birth control.

▶ *Is herpes as bad as everybody is saying it is?*

The severity of physical symptoms varies from person to person. In some people, the blisters and pain are acute and last for a relatively long time, while in other people the symptoms are mild and go away quickly. Some people have frequent recurrences, while others never experience an outbreak again.

We assume you're asking about the psychological effects of contracting a sexually transmitted disease which cannot, as of this date, be cured. The media have even referred to herpes sufferers as the "new lepers." We feel that while the *initial* shock of contracting herpes can be severe, most people recover and adjust well to the situation. Many of them marry and have children (though here medical precautions must be observed).

Within any relationships, the main factor is honesty: if you have herpes, tell any prospective partner the truth *before* having sexual relations. People who have herpes find that few partners reject them sexually for that reason alone.

► *Can you get STD more than once?*
Yes, you can be reinfected anytime you are cured of previous infections. You can also have more than one STD at a time.

► *How can you tell if you have gonorrhea?*
Gonorrhea usually shows up in men two to six days after sexual contact with an infected person. In some cases, it doesn't show up for a month or more. The first sign is usually pus dripping from the penis or a burning feeling while urinating. However, about 10 percent of the men who get gonorrhea show no signs at all. Just the same, the disease can be spreading through their bodies, and anyone who has sex with them is likely to become infected.

In women there may be a slight discharge from the vagina, accompanied by a burning feeling. However, most of the time there are no signs at all. A woman may not realize there is something wrong for weeks or months, or even years, after she was infected.

If gonorrhea remains untreated, it can cause sterility, arthritis, heart trouble and general bad health. Treatment at any public-health clinic is confidential and not subject to parental approval.

FERTILITY

► *Are many couples infertile and is science making progress in this area?*
It is estimated that there are in the United States about 10 million adults between the ages of eighteen and forty who ex-

perience difficulties in conceiving a child or carrying a pregnancy to term. Infertility is on the rise due to sexually transmitted disease, a tendency to postpone childbearing and many other still-unknown factors. Medical science continues to make slow but steady progress to assist couples who are finding it difficult to conceive.

When a woman is unable to conceive, we call her infertile. There can be several reasons. Her fallopian tubes may be blocked so the egg (ovum) necessary for fertilization does not descend. There may be a hormonal imbalance or other medical reasons. If a woman wishes to have a child but does not get pregnant, she should consult a physician who specializes in that field. Sometimes there are psychological reasons for failure to conceive. Psychotherapy can then be of help. Childlessness, of course, cannot always be attributed to the woman. A significant number of men are sterile—i.e., their sperm is unable to fertilize the egg. This can be determined by a physician who does a sperm count and analysis. If a couple have been unable to conceive, the male should be examined first because his examination is relatively simple and inexpensive.

CHAPTER TEN

STD–Sexually Transmitted Diseases

One of the most pressing areas in the entire field of human sexuality and, at the same time, one of the topics enveloped by ignorance and misinformation is venereal disease, now referred to as sexually transmitted disease (STD). Read the following four statements and decide whether each is true or false.

1. Syphilis and gonorrhea are the only serious venereal diseases in the United States.
2. STD can be transmitted only via genital contact.
3. Once the signs of STD disappear, the person is cured.
4. Once you contract STD you certainly know you have it.

All four statements are false. Most young people—and even most adults—would answer "True" to one or more of these statements, a dramatic illustration of how much work needs to be done sensitizing people to recognize the dangers of STD. Every parent should be well-informed on this topic, which we shall address in this chapter.

The United States Public Health Service's Center for Disease Control estimates that at least 10 to 15 million Americans contract a form of sexually transmitted disease each year. The annual medical cost of this disease is staggering: about one billion dollars. The emotional trauma suffered by afflicted individuals, as well as the strains it places on relationships, can hardly be measured. Sexually transmitted disease now constitutes the number-one reportable communicable disease in the United States. The problem is most serious among young adults, where the STD rate in the sixteen-to-twenty age group is *three times* the level of the general population.

The breadth and seriousness of venereal disease in the United States have led many researchers and educators to redefine the entire area of study. In fact the term "venereal disease" refers most directly to diseases contracted during sexual intercourse. Because many infections can be transmitted during other intimate body contacts, the preferred term is STD—i.e., diseases that are capable of being transmitted through contact with the genitals, the anus, the mouth and other body areas.

Some believe that this epidemic results from increased sexual promiscuity, ignorance, or professional and public apathy. Whether you agree with these theories or not, the fact remains that the available statistics are nothing short of shocking.

The U.S. Center for Disease Control in Atlanta estimated that there would be in 1986 the following new cases of sexually transmitted diseases: chlamydia, 3 million; gonorrhea, 1 million; condyloma (genital warts), 1 million; genital herpes, 500,000; and syphilis, 90,000.

Chlamydia and condyloma have replaced genital herpes as the new raging epidemics. Condyloma is a virus that breeds in the warm, moist tissues of the genital tract and causes cauliflowerlike warts. Antibiotics do not kill the growths, and the warts must be removed. Condyloma's favorite targets are fifteen- to twenty-five-year-olds. The most serious and tragic of all STDs is AIDS—a fatal disease which will claim as many as 20,000 victims by the end of 1986.

It is important to understand that STD refers to a wide range of diseases including but not limited to syphilis, gonorrhea, NGU and genital herpes. In fact, there are twelve diseases in addition to the commonly recognized venereal ones (syphilis and gonorrhea) that qualify as STDs. In this section we'll discuss briefly each of the important ones. We provide this information out of our strong conviction that knowledge promotes responsible behavior; conversely, ignorance of the methods of STD prevention and detection can potentially harm the individual's health and well-being. When someone suspects that he or she is infected with an STD, competent medical diagnosis and treatment must be sought. *Home remedies should not be attempted* and may serve only to complicate matters.

SYPHILIS

Syphilis is almost always spread by some form of sexual contact. We say "almost always" because some people might not think of kissing as sexual. There have been occasional cases where a person has caught the disease by open-mouth kissing with someone who had it.

Left untreated, syphilis can last for a person's lifetime. There are thousands of infected people who aren't aware of having it; they either were never treated or think they no longer have the disease. Untreated, syphilis can result in serious disabilities including paralysis, brain injury and insanity, heart disease and skin disease.

Syphilis can be detected and successfully treated by a physician. The drug of choice is penicillin, unless the individual is allergic to it, in which case synthetic antibiotics are prescribed. Any damage already done by the disease cannot be reversed. Thus the importance of early diagnosis and treatment is obvious, for even though the spirochete bacteria that cause syphilis may have been killed, a damaged heart will never regenerate.

It is important to remember that syphilis goes through three main stages. The first stage is usually signaled by the appearance of a sore called a chancre. It appears anywhere from ten to ninety days after the bacteria enter the body. The sore resembles a pimple or wart and may or may not produce pus. In men it usually appears on the penis. In women it usually shows up either on the labia or inside the vagina. The chancre produces neither pain nor itching and, especially among women, may go undetected if not visible. Chancres may appear in other places on the body where sexual contact was made, in an odd spot (on the arm or a toe), or simply not at all.

The second stage of the disease begins with the disappearance of sores. This does not signal a cure. From about two weeks to six months after the initial sexual contact, other signs (a rash, welts around the genitals, ugly sores in the armpits, between the toes or in the mouth, a low-grade fever, headaches, sore throat) make themselves known. These symptoms are sometimes attributed to other, less serious causes and may disappear and recur in some people. Eventually, in all victims they disappear.

A patient usually enters the third stage of syphilis about two years after initially contracting the disease. While still infected, the person is no longer infectious; the illness cannot be passed to another person. The one exception to this rule is a pregnant woman, who can pass the infection on to her fetus. An individual can feel quite healthy during this stage of the illness, but the infection continues to do more and more damage. During the next five years, the disease will probably affect the heart, the brain and other organs, ultimately causing both physical and mental crippling and possibly death.

GONORRHEA

Gonorrhea has been popularly known by many names: "the clap," "the drip," "a dose," "the whites," "morning drop" and other colloquialisms. Myths that some people have believed are that you can contract gonorrhea from lifting something heavy or from contact with toilet seats, doorknobs, dirty sheets and unwashed eating utensils.

A person contracts gonorrhea in almost all cases when the penis enters the vagina, the mouth or the rectum. Gonorrhea bacteria (gonococci) thrive in the type of tissue found in the urinary tract, the throat, the cervix and the rectum. The disease has a number of potentially dangerous results. Untreated gonorrhea is the most common cause of sterility in women. It can cause arthritis, heart disease and general poor health. Men who have had gonorrhea sometimes have difficulty urinating for the remainder of their lives. As is the case with syphilis, gonorrhea can be detected and successfully treated. An individual can contract the disease as many times as he or she comes into contact with another infected person.

Between three and six days after the gonococci enter the body, a man usually experiences a milky-white drip from the penis which may be accompanied by a burning sensation when urinating. Occasionally these signs don't appear until about a month after the initial contact. Furthermore, in some cases a large amount of pus may be discharged. In other cases, a male will notice only a slight, cloudy discharge in the morning. The burning feeling while urinating may be only a little uncomfortable, or it may be extremely painful. It is important to note that about 10 to 20 percent of males who contract gonorrhea show minor symptoms or no signs at all. Among women, there may be a slight discharge from the vagina along with a burning feeling, but 80 percent of the time there are no symptoms. Thus, a woman may not know she has contracted gonorrhea for weeks, months or even years after she has initially been infected.

As of this date the medical tests for the detection of gonorrhea are not completely reliable, particularly for women in the first stages of the illness. As the disease progresses, the tests become more accurate. For this reason, sexually active people who have more than one partner should be regularly tested for gonorrhea, whether or not they think they have it. This is particularly important in light of the fact that, as with syphilis, the symptoms of gonorrhea can disappear even without medical treatment. All the while, the disease is damaging the body.

NGU (NONGONOCOCCAL URETHRITIS)

According to the Center for Disease Control, NGU has quickly become a major national health problem. Actually, it has been with us for a long time. Its symptoms can be misleading; they also tend to show signs of fading away and may not be easily recognized by some physicians. Unlike other STDs such as gonorrhea and syphilis, NGU is still not considered a communicable disease that must be reported.

The bacterium *chlamydis trachomatis* causes about one half of all NGU cases. The remainder are attributable to other organisms and irritation. NGU occurs most frequently in the urethra, the tube that runs from the bladder through the penis, or to the urethral opening in women. The disease generates pus in this area and thus in some respects resembles gonorrhea. NGU can cause an infection in the male's sperm ducts, sometimes causing a "drip," and can cause sterility if left unchecked. Another result may be prostatitis, a disorder of the prostate gland. Unchecked NGU in women may possibly cause sterility. Furthermore, NGU can attack newborn babies and cause pneumonia and eye infections; numerous stillborn deaths are blamed on NGU. Luckily, as with gonorrhea and syphilis, NGU can be successfully treated with antibiotics.

GENITAL HERPES

There are two types of herpes viruses. Type 1 appears most frequently on the lips. Type 2, or herpes simplex, occurs most frequently in the genital area, though each can occur in either location, and can be transferred from one part of the body to another by touching. Type 2, genital herpes, is almost always a sexually transmitted disease.

No cure for genital herpes exists at this time. A new medication being introduced, however, promises relief of the symptoms of the first outbreak of the virus. The medication is called Acyclovir, and at the time this book was written it was available only in a topical ointment. Researchers emphasize that the new medication is not a cure and is effective mainly against the symptoms of the initial outbreak. Thus the real hope lies in prevention. Here communication serves as our best line of defense.

The visible signs of genital herpes will appear very shortly after the initial contact, perhaps as quickly as one or two days. For women, the first experience of the disease will last about three weeks; the sores usually are very painful and are accompanied by flulike symptoms such as fever and headaches; then the disease enters a latent stage. For men, the first episode is somewhat shorter, perhaps two weeks, and the symptoms are somewhat less severe. In both men and women genital herpes usually reappears, although in later episodes the symptoms may be less severe than in the first one. These recurrences may be quite irregular and, perhaps, happen during periods of stress.

The seriousness of herpes is appreciated only when looking at the broader picture. At present, a person who contracts herpes is infected for an entire lifetime. Researchers have discovered that herpes increases a woman's chances of developing cervical cancer. Furthermore, a woman with an *active* case of genital herpes can infect her child at the time of delivery. Statistics show that in about half of these cases the infant will be infected, and about half of those infants will die. For this reason, many women who have herpes elect to deliver by Caesarean section just to be safe.

VAGINITIS

This is a common complaint among women. Vaginitis can be caused by a variety of different organisms, which may or may not be transmitted through sexual contact. Symptoms include a vaginal discharge, itchiness and an unpleasant odor. Medications can cure it, and treatment may last up to a month. There are, however, a number of steps which women can take in order to help prevent its occurrence:

1. Wear only cotton underpants (or at least underpants with a cotton crotch). Synthetic materials (nylon, etc.) keep moisture in and provide an ideal environment for the growth of vaginitis-causing organisms.
2. Wash the vulva and dry it thoroughly each day.
3. Never use feminine-hygiene sprays. These can irritate the vagina. If you sense that your vagina has an unusually strong or unpleasant odor, this may be an indication that you have an infection of some sort.
4. Always wipe with toilet paper from front to back, whether after urinating or after defecating. Wiping from the anus toward the vagina can transmit bacteria into the vagina which can cause infection.
5. When pants are worn, they should be relatively loose-fitting. Pants that are too tight in the crotch may cause irritations in the vulva and will also retain moisture.
6. Occasional (and only occasional) douching with a mildly acidic solution can help prevent vaginitis (use one or two tablespoons of vinegar in a quart of water).
7. Don't consume excessive amounts of sugar or carbohydrates.

OTHER STDs

There are a number of other STDs parents should be aware of which can pose a serious health threat to their children.

Trichomonas vaginalis involves an infection of the vagina, although men are also susceptible to infection. For this reason partners should be treated simultaneously—otherwise they will pass the disease back and forth between them (the Ping-Pong effect). Currently, it is estimated that there are about 2.3 million cases of this disease in the United States annually. It is especially common in women between the ages of sixteen and thirty-five. Often the only sign is a discharge with pus, though it may become painful and give off a noticeable odor. Although we classify this disease as an STD, it is possible to contract it nonsexually by coming into contact with an infected person's clothing or towel.

Chlamydia are organisms which are related to both bacteria and viruses. It is believed that they cause much of the vaginitis in women and NGU in men; it can also lead to PID (discussed below). Treatment of this infection usually consists of an antibiotic (most often tetracycline). Chlamydia infections are very widespread today, although it is difficult to measure exactly how many people are affected (chlamydia is not a reportable disease by law, although it is estimated that as many as one million people are affected each year).

Pelvic Inflammatory Disease (PID, also called *salpingitis*) is a severe infection of the female reproductive system. Usually the infection is caused by complications arising from, or failure to treat, another STD (such as gonorrhea or chlamydia). This infection starts in the vagina or cervix, then moves through the uterus and up into the fallopian tubes, sometimes reaching the ovaries.

Symptoms include pain and tenderness in the lower abdomen, painful urination, vaginal discharge, out-of-cycle menstrual bleeding and/or cramps, chills and fever. Early diagnosis and treatment with antibiotics is essential with PID: hospitalization, surgery and even death occur in women with severe cases. Sometimes women become infertile due to these infections; women who use the IUD need to be especially alert to the symptoms mentioned above, as they are ten times more likely to develop PID as women who use other forms of contraception.

Venereal warts are caused by a virus. They usually develop on the genitals three to five months after initial exposure. It is important to seek treatment quickly, as venereal warts may spread or enlarge and thus require surgical removal.

Crabs, also known as pubic lice, are tiny parasites that live in the pubic hair. Itching, caused by the lice attaching themselves to the skin, is the main symptom. Treatment is available through application of a medicated shampoo prescribed by a physician. After treatment, it is important to use a complete change of clothing and linens to avoid the possibility of reinfection.

Scabies are tiny mites that burrow under the skin, usually of the inner thighs and genitals. Scabies are transmitted by genital and other types of close contact with an infected person. A small group of open sores resulting from scratching is symptomatic of scabies. The treatment of choice usually is medicated shampoo. As with lice, the sexual partner should be checked and treated at the same time to avoid reinfestation. Clothing and bedding should also be changed.

Chancroid. Symptoms include a painful sore (or sores) on the genitals, followed by pain in the crotch area. Chancroid sometimes appears together with another STD, particularly herpes or syphilis. Tetracycline or other antibiotic is the usual treatment; women especially need to be cautious, because they often show no signs of infection.

Hepatitis is a viral infection of the liver which has symptoms of nausea, loss of appetite, fever, abdominal discomfort and pain in the joints. Hepatitis is sexually transmitted through oral-anal contact as well as anal intercourse. Treatment consists of a carefully controlled diet and prolonged bed rest.

Several other infections are also transmitted through sexual contact with the anus and rectum. These include shigellosis, amebiasis and giardiasis—also called "gay bowel disease." People with these infections suffer from irritation of the bowels, cramps, diarrhea and irregular bowel movements. AIDS (Acquired Immune Deficiency Syndrome) is a relatively recent discovery of medical science. The condition was isolated by physicians in 1979. Current research suggests that AIDS is spread mainly by anal sex.

AIDS is a condition in which the body's immune system stops protecting the individual against disease. This leaves the person vulnerable to cancer and various infections which the body can no longer defend against. It is believed that AIDS is caused by a virus or similar organism (not bacteria), and that it is spread in bodily fluids, especially blood and semen.

AIDS has been most prevalent among male homosexuals, although it has also infected some heterosexuals, intravenous drug users, and people who have received blood transfusions, particularly hemophiliacs. To date, doctors cannot cure it, and much further research is needed before they understand how to treat AIDS victims.

PARENTS, CHILDREN AND STDs

What should parents tell their children about STDs? First, let us express our conviction that the best time to learn about STDs is before becoming sexually active. If your children are already sexually active, it becomes even more urgent that they learn how to protect themselves. STDs such as gonorrhea or NGU pass from person to person about as rapidly and easily as the common cold.

More teenagers get STDs these days than ever before. Aside from abstinence, the condom is the best means of prevention available. Various other contraceptive methods provide little or no protection, and the pill tends to make women more susceptible. People can also decrease their chances of contracting VD by urinating and washing their genitals with soap and water immediately after sexual relations. Some young people simply do not worry about STDs because they know that, for the most part, a cure is available. These same youngsters forget that in order to be cured you must know that you have it in the first place. Thus we stress the value of information and open discussion of these matters between parents and children.

Parents as well as teenagers should be aware of the following signs of STDs. Parents might want their teenagers to read the following two paragraphs themselves. In general, a woman should seek medical help if she has any of the following signs:

• Burning while urinating.
• A persistent sore throat.

- Pain or itchiness in or around the vagina.
- Any soreness or redness around the vulva or the anus.
- Any sores, warts or pimples in or near the vulva.
- A discharge that is yellow, green or otherwise discolored. (A normal discharge is usually clear or milky.)
- A thick discharge that looks like cottage cheese.

In general, a man should seek medical help if he has any of the following signs:

- A persistent sore throat.
- Burning during and shortly after urination.
- Any sores, warts or pimples on the penis or around it.
- Any unusual coloring of the urine, such as urine which is reddish or very dark.
- A milky or puslike discharge.
- Any soreness or redness around the anus.

Immediate treatment is paramount if one should contract an STD. Adolescents will be more likely to seek treatment if parents stress that the subject of STD is open for discussion. In case your child might be too embarrassed to confide in you, make him or her aware of the numerous community resources in this field. It is essential to stress that diagnosis can be made only by microscopic examination. Tell your teenage children that treatment is confidential. Local health centers, STD clinics, the county health department, the local office of Planned Parenthood, family-planning clinics, hospital clinics or your private physician are all options. Parental consent for minors is not required, and treatment is often free of charge.

There is a national, toll-free number which is an important resource for those seeking information. VD Hotline provides information and referrals to locally available treatment centers. Its number is 800-227-8922. (For California residents the number is 800-982-5883.)

There is a great deal of truth to the old adage "An ounce of prevention is worth a pound of cure." The most significant message parents can teach their children is to prevent themselves from becoming infected in the first place. Parents may not want their teenage children to engage in any form of sexual activity, but they should give their children the information necessary to protect themselves if they choose to have sex against their parents' wishes.

Every male and female must be taught the responsibility to wash genital and rectal areas before and after sex contact, reducing acquired germs and secretions and one's own, in protection of one's health and that of one's sex partner.

Society could help reduce the incidence of STDs by promoting the notion that they are not a cause for stigma; they are simply diseases that happen to be spread by sexual contact.

Refocusing society's attitudes, and laying to rest some of the social taboos that long have clouded understanding of this topic, would help people feel more comfortable in seeking treatment. Any sexually active person can contract an STD. Many young people feel that only other individuals will get it, not themselves. This may be particularly true for young women, as STDs have traditionally been regarded as "male diseases." The double standard operates here. Society accepts—perhaps unintentionally encourages—STDs as part of the male image. For adolescent girls, planning to prevent an STD suggests sexual premeditation, an idea which can seem more threatening than the possibility of infection itself.

The condom exists as a simple, convenient, reliable, inexpensive method of both birth control and prevention of STDs. Yet with the recent revolution in contraception (the pill, the IUD, the diaphragm), the condom has fallen into disfavor. The incidence of STDs among our population, especially young people, has increased during these same years. For example, the fifteen-to-nineteen-year-old group now accounts for 25 percent of all reported gonorrhea. The Center for Disease Control reported that in 1981 over 300,000 cases of gonorrhea actually occurred among young females. These cases developed into an estimated 45,000 incidents of pelvic inflammatory disease, a severe complication of untreated STD, which left between 7,000 and 18,000 of its victims sterile. Perhaps the United States should follow the lead of Japan, where the condom remains the most frequently used form of birth control.

The tireless efforts of clinics, Planned Parenthood and related agencies to educate the public have not really permeated the

THE STDs: ANOTHER WAY OF LOOKING AT IT*

Danger Signs	Could Be	Complications
Common male signs: Discharge from penis; Soreness inside penis; Burning on urination; Rectal irritation and pus; Swelling or redness of throat; Yellow discharge from penis	Gonorrhea; NGU; Other genital infections that also need medical attention	Untreated gonorrhea can cause sterility, arthritis, heart trouble and blindness. Repeated infections can cause partial or complete blockage of the penis.
Common female signs: Gray offensive vaginal discharge; Thick and profuse vaginal discharge; Intense itching; Painful intercourse; Thick cheesy discharge; Rectal irritation, and pus covering feces; Swelling or redness of throat; Out-of-cycle stomach cramps; Unusual vaginal or cervical bleeding	Gonorrhea; Nonspecific vaginitis; Trichomonas; Monilia (yeast)	If untreated, gonorrhea can cause pelvic inflammatory disease which resembles appendicitis. This causes severe pain, fever, sterility, arthritis and heart trouble.
Common signs for both sexes: Painless sore on penis or vagina; Painful sore or blisters on or around genital area; Rash on hands and feet or entire body; Loss of hair; Small cauliflower-pink growths on or around sex organs; Intense itching; Flulike feeling	Syphilis; Herpes virus; Hepatitis; Scabies; Crabs; Venereal warts	Untreated syphilis can cause brain and other organ damage; also paralysis, blindness, heart disease and death. The most severe complication of herpes genitalis is infection of the newborn during birth, which can be fatal.

* Courtesy Florida State Department of Health and Rehabilitative Services.

mainstream of American life. Television, with the exception of a very few local stations, refuses to advertise condoms. Rules regulating the display and advertisement of over-the-counter contraceptives are all too restrictive. Schools do not generally offer information on STDs. Without decisive measures, society effectively condemns many of its young people to unnecessary harm.

CHAPTER ELEVEN

Fostering a Child's Sexual Integrity in Special Situations

The Census Bureau estimates that more than half of the children born in 1980 will spend a substantial part of their first eighteen years in a single-parent home. In 1985 there were close to 15 million single parents in the United States.

THE SINGLE PARENT

The ordinary problems encountered in two-parent households may become magnified when there is only one person to face them. There is an abundance of existing literature advising single parents of the unique difficulties involved, the trials of day care, financial woes, etc. The problems are not nearly as insurmountable as was once assumed, however, and in many instances a special bond develops between children and their single mother or father. One or two parents is not the issue; rather, the quality of love and care the child receives in the home will determine his or her overall adjustment and well-being.

Single parents who worry that their children will grow up psychologically impaired should know that there is no evidence that single-parent families produce traumatized children any more than that the conventional two-parent family guarantees emotional stability. Children are amazingly resilient and resourceful. They will understandably be hurt by divorce or by the death of a parent; this is essentially a healthy response to grief. In such situations, it is most important to reassure your children that they are still loved, and that they are *in no way responsible for the absence of the other parent.* Young children are apt to feel "It's my fault that Daddy died" or "If I was good, Mommy wouldn't have left." Older children might cover up an inner sense of guilt by harboring bitter feelings: "If Dad loved me, he would have stayed." Children in these instances will not respond to vague consolation. The single parent must tell the child, in the case of divorce, that the parents did not get along. If it's appropriate, the reasons can be explained, but in general it's not a good idea to reveal details of sexual incompatibility or other highly personal motives. On the other hand, it is probably unwise to attempt to conceal the "other" man or woman if there is one. These facts have a way of becoming obvious over time, and inadvertently finding out about them may violate the child's sense of trust.

If the absent parent abandoned the family, suggestions that the absent parent still loves them can only confuse and upset the children. If the abandoner has lost interest or found another home, the children might be encouraged to accept the reality of it, instead of pretending for years that the parent may be coming back or "thinks of you all the time." Assurances of enduring love are called for only if they have some credibility. In general, it is best to be honest about the circumstances of single-parenthood and to encourage the children to accept them realistically.

In many instances, the single-parent home is a more desirable situation for the children than the two-parent home. If a couple have been plagued by endless battles and bitter feelings, children often fare better when the war is finally ended. The child's sexual identity will not necessarily suffer without the appropriate male or female role model. There's an abundance of role models among relatives, schoolteachers and parents of friends.

It is to be hoped that agreeable arrangements have been

worked out between ex-spouses concerning child care and visitation rights and the payment of alimony and child support. A high level of conflict typically surrounds divorce proceedings, and the children often become enmeshed in it. Parents sometimes use their children as pawns in the power struggle, playing loyalties against each other and demanding that the child state with which parent he or she prefers to live. This is damaging to the child, whose right it is to continue to love and be loved by both parents.

Most single parents do not live with their lovers, but the majority do have ongoing relationships and/or sexual encounters. According to researcher Morton Hunt, within the first year of separation five out of six individuals become sexually active again. The single parent can live a sexual existence and still appear responsible and stable to the children. In fact, the situation presents an opportunity to show children that "sexuality" and "responsibility" go hand in hand.

Children may at first feel somewhat threatened or jealous of the parent's interest in another partner. There may be feelings of loyalty to the parent no longer at home, or the desire to protect the parent from getting emotionally hurt in the new affair. These feelings are apt to be stronger if the child feels left out, so it's a good idea to involve the child in whatever card games, conversation or recreation is going on. When the child begins to suspect that your feelings for this new person are important, he or she may likely ask if you have plans to remarry, or if your feelings for each other are serious. Children need and deserve honesty at this stage; parents can acknowledge their feelings without feeling compelled to cover up or make excuses.

In the early stages of their sexual relationships, most people confine their sexual activities to times when the children are either asleep or not home, or they go to the other person's house or apartment. Our view is that unless there is a sense of continuation to the relationship, it is best not to spend the night together in the house while the children are there. It can be very difficult for the child to adapt to a new lover every so often, if that is the single parent's lifestyle. There may come a time in more ongoing relationships, however, when it becomes very inconvenient and enervating to arrange constantly for sexual relations outside the home. The parent can then weigh the child's needs and likely reaction against his or her own desires for intimacy.

The decision is likely to be easier if the child has accepted the boyfriend or girlfriend and seems to like the person. It is often the case, in fact, that children develop deep emotional ties to these other partners and consequently suffer a sense of loss if the relationship ends. The children may welcome the camaraderie of having another person in the house and appreciate the positive effect on the parent. Sex itself thus becomes a secondary issue, and it yields in significance to other intricate considerations that come with living under the same roof. It is not uncommon for children to press the parent to marry, which of course should not influence the parent's decision—although if marriage is contemplated, it's good to know how the children feel.

In the early stages of any new relationship, it's best if the role of parent and disciplinarian remains solely with the parent. Children often resent the interference of a boyfriend or girlfriend, rightfully so, and may retort with "Leave me alone—you're not my parent." As the relationship progresses, children may welcome the advice and guidance of another adult, which they see as prevalent in their friends' two-parent households. Some people who have no children of their own, however, do not feel comfortable with children and have no idea how to relate to them. In an unhappy situation, the parent may be confronted with a child's ultimatum, "Either he goes or I do." It's very important to be sensitive to the child's feelings and not automatically assume he or she is just acting spoiled or selfish. The parent might respond, "I love you both differently, but I can't let you make my decisions for me. You'll always be my child no matter what happens, and I'm not sure what the future holds for my lover and me. But you and I will always love each other—and that's the difference."

Deprived of a second parent, a child usually will find another adult to relate closely with. It may be a teacher, a coach, a relative, or a Boy or Girl Scout leader. A volunteer from the Big Brothers or Big Sisters program can be very helpful. The person may adopt the role of "significant other" or may simply provide the child with a measure of closeness and friendship. It is a good idea for the single parent to encourage and support these liaisons. One-parent households sometimes have a tendency to turn inward, cutting off important interaction with the outside world. It is common that an extraordinary bond of love and closeness develops between children and parent in such circumstances, but it shouldn't be so exclusive that it becomes a stifling case of "you and me against the world."

The ongoing responsibility of sex-educating the child can be assumed by the single parent for children of both sexes. Children appreciate their own parent's candor and openness, but if the parent is too uncomfortable discussing sexual issues perhaps a relative or close friend might be willing to fill in. Single fathers may want to seek female assistance to demonstrate how to manage a sanitary napkin before the onset of a daughter's menstruation. All other matters pertaining to sexuality can be sensitively and competently handled by single parents of either sex.

Single parents are correct in assuming that their child's sexuality and needs are no different from those in two-parent homes. The children require the same anatomical, contraceptive, behavioral and attitudinal information imparted to all youngsters. Discipline and guidance are just as crucial, and no special allowances need be made because the child has only one parent.

SEXUAL HEALTH AND THE DISABLED CHILD

A while ago one of the authors was addressing a meeting of several hundred individuals who have severe disabilities, with their parents and related health professionals. After an enthusiastic half-hour presentation, the gathering remained sullen and unimpressed. The speaker had talked positively of the rights of all individuals to sexual expression and intimate relationships, and yet the audience did not respond. Finally there was an emotional outburst from one workshop leader. She shouted, "How can you say things like that when you see before you people who need only look at themselves in the mirror to know that what you say represents empty promises of a future that is not possible for any of them!"

The answer came from a woman confined to a wheelchair. She said, "You know, when I look only at myself, I feel depressed. When I take in the world I live in, I'm impressed. And when I allow God to touch me, I feel blessed."

Pandemonium broke out. The formerly unreceptive, frustrated crowd became a group of people wanting desperately to talk about their hidden aspirations, mainly in terms of their strong desires for love, companionship and sexual expression.

Society has conspired to deny individuals with disabling conditions their inherent sexual nature. Parents, as well as institutions to which handicapped people may be confined, have responded to the rehabilitative and educational needs of the disabled in all major areas save that of sexuality. A victim of an automobile accident who is suddenly paraplegic, a child born cerebral-palsied, and others with a variety of handicapping conditions are taught how to handle the orthopedic devices, wheelchairs, prosthetics and other special adaptations that are required. In many cases, extraordinary inventiveness has been displayed in overcoming tremendous difficulties. In the area of life that people most yearn for regardless of their physical or mental incapacities, however, little effort has been made.

The handicaps these individuals live with have been allowed to overshadow all other areas of their existence. Parents of a teenager who is paralyzed from the waist down tend to assume that their child's sexual feelings are also extinguished. Families of young people who have congenital brain injury or spinal-cord damage, or who are blind or deaf or suffer from other handicaps often make the same faulty assumptions: my child has enough to worry about without all the pressures and potential for failure associated with sex.

Most individuals with disabilities suffer from extremely low levels of self-esteem. They look into the mirror and see deformed limbs or spastic and uncontrolled body movements, and they worry, "How could anyone ever love me?" Those with mentally handicapping conditions also fear that they are unattractive to other people. Perhaps they have already failed in school or been relegated to special classes or have had to face the fact that they will never be able to hold a job or live a normal life. Isolated from the rest of society by physical barriers and often spending the majority of their time at home or in an institution, they see little hope for the future.

Despite the enormous difficulties they face, it is time for parents to think about their handicapped children in these terms: "Yes, we want you to love and be loved. Yes, we want you to express your sexuality in whatever ways are possible for you, and we will support your wishes to that end." Apart from the obvious difficulties their handicaps pose, the main problems these young people have are usually a lack of friends, companionship and things to do that are interesting to them, and frustration of their sexual needs. The handicap itself can emerge as a minor problem compared to their feelings of worthlessness and despair.

Information is a first and most powerful ally. For instance, being unfamiliar with the ordinary obscenities young people use can make a disabled person the brunt of coarse jokes. Young people who are handicapped and from whom sexual information is kept secret, who are discouraged from asking questions, scolded for experimentation, shamed for being found out and denied both the privacy and the social opportunities to explore their natural sexuality, will probably suffer more than would "normal" children under the same circumstances. The self-image suffers tremendously from the handicap; being denied the right to information and the freedom to express their sexuality magnifies these burdens unbearably.

The sexual needs of individuals with handicaps are no different from those of the rest of the population. Physiologically, there may be catheters to deal with, braces to be removed or transitory sensation in their genitals. They may have to struggle out of wheelchairs or cope with shaky hands, and may slur the intimate words they speak to each other. These are secondary considerations to what goes on in their hearts and minds.

Their birthright to full sexual expression, however, is accompanied by the same responsibilities that apply to any other person. Teenagers with disabilities are also too young and too vulnerable to experience sexual intercourse, and they must be as careful to guard against pregnancy and STD as their nonhandicapped counterparts. They must be as sensitive to other people's feelings as "normal" youngsters.

There is evidence to suggest that parents of handicapped youth spend more time than other parents in discouraging their children's masturbation. This can be an especially devastating restriction for the handicapped adolescent, who often does not have the opportunities for socializing, dating, kissing, hand holding, etc., available to other teenagers. Many institutions spend inordinate amounts of energy to guarantee that patients do not even have enough privacy to masturbate. Any person who is prohibited from exploring his or her sexuality in this way, and is made to feel guilty about it, may suffer a variety of emotional consequences. As we state unequivocally in our discussion of masturbation, it is a normal sexual expression for people of any age, provided it is voluntary and enjoyable. For people who do not have sufficient motor control to masturbate themselves, vibrators can be used with satisfying results.

Some young people with disabilities seem to masturbate a great deal, which is often a response to boredom or lack of outside interests. This is usually not a sexual problem *per se*. The solution, if the behavior really is excessive, is to stimulate the youngster in other ways and provide social experiences and interaction that satisfy the need for human relationships.

Handicapped young people sometimes need their parents' assistance in arranging dates or finding opportunities to meet other young people. If they cannot run down the street to meet their friends, or get to high-school dances under their own steam, they will need help. Parents are usually willing to make extra efforts to get their handicapped youngsters out of the house so that their child will not miss out on valuable socializing experiences. What is missing is programs to meet the needs of handicapped people.

Sometimes a parent discourages a disabled youngster from dating or going to high-school dances or parties for fear the child will be hurt or rebuffed. That is certainly an understandable fear. Yet to deny the child an opportunity to get dressed up and go out and take a chance, even to risk getting hurt and feeling heartbroken, is to deny him or her a major experience in living.

Disabled youth and adults want to socialize as much as other people. Since adolescents generally have far more social experience with members of their own sex, they tend to feel nervous and anxious about their first dating experiences. This is especially true for those with obvious physical impairments which make them feel unattractive and fear rejection. For this reason, double-dating or group activities are often preferable and easier in the beginning.

A young girl worried about her appearance, for example, would feel more comfortable in a mixed group. When all the girls excuse themselves for a conference in the bathroom, she could join them and share in the general concern over hairstyles and lipstick. It may give her renewed confidence to see that the other girls have just as many uncertainties as she does. To the best of their abilities, disabled adolescents should care for their appearance; grooming, manners and appropriate clothing all help. They should realize that no matter how hard they try to please, some people will find them unattractive, others won't seem to care, and still others will find in them a singular beauty.

Sometimes young people with disabilities become so immersed in self-pity that they decide in advance nobody will ever love them or want to marry them. The alternative to making such grim prophecies and waiting for time to bear them out is to find or create new reasons to love and respect oneself. Positive self-regard is what counts: "If I look as if I am mightily enjoying my own company, chances are somebody else will soon be along wishing to share it."

As teenagers mature in their social relationships, they may begin to think seriously about marriage. Popular mythology notwithstanding, many disabled persons do marry and adjust quite successsfully. A few prefer to remain single; the problem is with those who would like to marry but who fear that their impairment makes them ineligible. If your child wishes to marry another disabled person, you may worry about being saddled with yet another financial burden. Yet parents who have already accepted permanent financial responsibility for one disabled child may find that with the help of a second set of parents their share of supporting two is less expensive. There will be others to share shopping, laundry and chauffeuring, rent, utilities and phone bills. Moreover, with new feelings of independence, and with the energy generated by a loving relationship, the disabled partners may become less dependent emotionally on their respective parents.

Adults with disabilities who want to have children may be confronted with objections from doctors and parents. In this situation, one cannot talk blithely of the right to bear offspring, or the joys of nurturance and comfort a child might bring to the couple. Romantic fantasies about parenthood abound—cuddling sweet sleeping infants while they gurgle delightedly, and loving them to pieces with never a scream in the middle of the night, and never a rash, an emergency or two weeks of diarrhea. The best approach is to evaluate realistically whether the couple are able to care for a child. There are added expenses to be considered, as well as the child's need and right to be raised in a stimulating environment. Those who think they would like to have a child but aren't sure of their ability to manage might volunteer to work in a nursery or a day-care center for a while to get an idea of what is involved. It's not a foolproof precaution, but it can be instructive.

Marriage for adults with disabilities is often more successful without children, without the inevitable disruption and strain involved in child rearing. Other drawbacks include the possibility that a normal child born of mentally retarded parents may subsequently become retarded as a consequence of inferior care and insufficient stimulation during the formative years. It is difficult for even a mildly retarded couple to understand the future implications of having a child and providing years of care; more commonly a mentally disabled husband and wife will tend to focus on the present, the pleasures and satisfactions of the moment, at the expense of hard thinking about tomorrow's consequences and responsibilities.

In some cases voluntary sterilization (vasectomy for the male, tubal ligation for the female) may be the best answer for seriously disabled couples, for those who couldn't possibly expect to cope with parenthood or for those who are certain that they do not, and never will, wish to have children. Sterilization should be considered as permanent and therefore inappropriate for anyone who is uncertain about choosing a childless lifestyle.

An unplanned or unwanted pregnancy can mean exceptional hardship for the disabled, from coping with the rigors of pregnancy to caring for the child after it is born. In such cases abortion may be a solution.

Lest the foregoing seem to stress parental responsibilities at the expense of parental rights to "live a little," too, let it be understood that parents owe it to themselves and to their children to find time for their own needs. Selfless devotion is neither possible nor desirable. Guilt is no excuse for directing every bit of energy to a life other than one's own. Parents of handicapped children frequently have the notion, conscious or unconscious, that they are somehow to blame for their child's affliction. Unable to relieve themselves of such misplaced guilt, they "punish" themselves by reorganizing their lives so that the disabled child is always at the center. There are many consequences of such thinking, nearly all negative. Storybook perfection is fine for storybook people. Real children, whether disabled or not, need their mothers and fathers to know when it is time to stop sacrificing and be unafraid to say so.

SEX EDUCATION PROGRAMS
FOR PERSONS WITH DISABILITIES

The basic principles which apply to a well-structured sex education program for the "normal" child apply also to the handicapped child; the goals are the same. The disabled are equally curious about "where they came from," differences between the sexes, changes at puberty, mate selection, dating, love, premarital sex, marriage, homosexual relations, masturbation and contraception.

There are special considerations for handicapped adolescents, commensurate with their particular disability. Sex education for the retarded is best presented in simple terms with considerable repetition. For the blind, more emphasis is placed on tactility; the use of dolls with genitals is preferable to neutered dolls, and rubber models similar to those used by medical schools are available. For the deaf, a visual emphasis is most beneficial; materials with drawings of male and female anatomies, prenatal development, birth and contraceptive information are necessary. Young adults with catheters, ostomies, braces or other special devices must be instructed on how to adapt themselves sexually. Film presentations portraying disabled people and their need to give and receive affection are available. It should be noted that the sexuality of a handicapped person might not conform to a parent's or society's view of sex as genital contact leading to orgasm. Special people need special, creative ideas and attitudes, and it is cruel to compound their difficulties because we may not be comfortable with the fact that they are indeed able and anxious to express sensual, sexual feelings.

Here are a few messages for people who have handicaps, especially those who are feeling sorry for themselves.

In our society you score no points for being disabled. Every person who has a disability has to struggle to make it.

1. Nobody can make you feel inferior without your consent.
2. If you have an interest (hobbies, work, talents, passions) someone will be interested in you.
3. If you are bored, you are boring to be with.
4. If you do not have a sense of humor, cultivate one.
5. Join an advocacy group for the handicapped.
6. Do not dwell on the meaning of life. Life is not a meaning. Life is an opportunity for any number of meaningful experiences.
7. Read. Discover as much as you can about yourself and the world. For heaven's sake, do not watch more than a couple of hours of television each day. Haven't you noticed that the more television you watch, the more exhausted you are?
8. Operate on the assumption that the so-called general public is uncomfortable with you. Most people are uncomfortable in the presence of people who have handicaps. Usually, if you tell them they do not have to feel guilty about feeling uncomfortable, they will respond.

We feel that these "rules" are the basic steps toward realizing your own goals. Nothing we have suggested is easy. In fact, all really meaningful experiences in life involve risk, hard work and the ability to postpone momentary gratification for long-range satisfaction. If you are able to feel good about yourself, someone will feel good about you. If you feel friendly, someone will be friendly to you. If you are open to sexual expression, someone will want to be sexual with you.

CHAPTER TWELVE

The Family Is Alive and Getting Better

A new family today holds more promise than its traditional predecessor, mainly due to the influence exerted by women's liberation, a movement which has created a great deal of turbulence in our society. We see it as a healthy, exciting and enriching opportunity for both men and women, one that will, in redefining family life, prevent it from self-destructing.

If there is a problem, it stems from society's resistance—from both males and females—to the legitimate demands of an increasingly large number of women, supported by a smaller but growing number of men. The demands are both simple and straightforward: equal opportunity in decision-making, career choice and leisure-time activities, and equal pay for equal work.

I, Sol Gordon, did not understand any of this when Judith and I were married thirty years ago. Judith, a busy professional, working full time, did all the cooking, cleaning, washing, shopping, cleaning, cooking, shopping, taking care of our child, shopping, cleaning, washing . . . I was busy. Until one day not too far along in our marriage my wife said to me, "I'm busy, too. How would you like to do all the work?" It took me five minutes to rearrange my schedule. I still don't like to help with the cooking and the housework, but I'm doing it—and our relationship has become much more mature and more full as a result of our sharing. Let's look at a few current trends in American family life, based on statistics available from the United States Census Bureau.

The family is by no means dead. Ninety-two percent of all Americans eventually marry, although a majority will not do so until their middle twenties. Only 25 percent of first marriages end in divorce or desertion. About 75 percent of these people remarry.

Eighty percent of all noninstitutionalized children under the age of eighteen live with two parents. Sixty-three percent of these reside with both natural parents of a first marriage. Twenty percent live in one-parent families. Though some couples decide not to have any children, the majority of married couples still have two or more.

More than 50 percent of all women with children now work outside the home. The good old American family consisting of a working father and a mother who stays at home caring for two children accounts for only 7 percent of the total. Clearly, we need to stop placing "guilt trips" on women who get others to take care of their children while they go off to work. No credible evidence proves that children who are in day care grow up more disturbed than those whose parents stay at home to take care of them. Though there are many studies which imply this proposition, none has been able to document the fact that children cared for during the day by nursery schools, grandparents, etc., are harmed by the process. We know of many such situations where children have grown into healthy, mature adults. We know of many instances where the mothers never worked outside the home, yet their children didn't fare too well. It seems strange that the very people who fuss about the importance of primary parental care often have careers and make use of expensive baby-sitters and housekeepers.

A much more ominous fact concerns the one million cases of child abuse in this country each year. Parents brutalize 100,000 of these children so severely that they require hospitalization. Furthermore, between 2,000 and 4,000 children are murdered by their parents every year. Virtually all of these parents are full-time caretakers of their children.

We see violence as a tragic byproduct of a family life that stresses the traditional roles of the authoritarian male and the submissive female. The frustration and anxiety generated by these forced roles often lead to family violence among spouses, and consequently the children become the innocent victims of their parents' rage.

In her book *Battered Women*, Lenore Walker stated:

Sexism is the real underbelly of human suffering. Men fight with other men to prove they are not "sissies" like women. Women show passive faces to the world while struggling to keep their lives together without letting men know how strong they are for fear of hurting their men's masculine image. And men beat women up in order to keep themselves on top of this whole messy heap. Little girls and little boys learn these sex-role expectations through early socialization. Unless we strive for equal power relations between men and women, women will continue to be victims of assaults . . .

The period of transition from traditional to egalitarian family through which we now are passing will exact a price. Not all men will be able to interact on an emotional level with their families, and their attempts at domestic chores may be fumbling and awkward. Not all women will be able to balance a successful career with marriage and a family. The baby-versus-career issue is an imperative one for the 1980s. How will a woman achieve equality with men in the marketplace if she chooses to also have children? Betty Friedan has addressed this important question in her recent book entitled *The Second Stage*.

Many such dilemmas face women these days. Many professions to which women have gained access over the past few decades simply are not structured for those who want to take a year off to have children. Some jobs take such a heavy toll in time and energy that a woman simply cannot see her way clear to having children in the first place. A cruel choice faces women of approximately thirty-five years who have spent ten years building a career for themselves and who now are on the verge of achieving a position of status or power. They fast approach the age when it becomes less safe to bear children. Do they sacrifice children or career? On the other hand, it must be noted that a surprisingly large number of women have successfully combined full-time careers with having families.

As more and more women become seriously involved with their careers, the very nature of family decisions is changing. It used to be assumed (and sometimes still is) that when the male received a promotion to a better job in another city, the family moved. Now the father is more likely to ask his family if they *want* to move. More and more men are rejecting promotions tied to relocations if moving is contrary to the family's welfare. Today it is not unheard of for the family to move for the wife's career advancement.

Egalitarian marriage is characterized by the couple's genuine respect for each other. Equal is not at issue; equal opportunity is. Each person maintains respect for the other's qualities and imperfections, affording each partner the opportunity to develop to the fullest potential. Men are beginning to show their appreciation for this type of relationship.

Although the double standard remains a pervasive force in this country, many changes have occurred. We examined articles in *The Ladies' Home Journal* written about thirty years ago and compared them with articles in the same magazine published this year. Formerly, the articles concentrated on how women should make their husbands happy. The following words of advice were typical:

> Love him. Unconditionally and with devotion. You chose him. He must be wonderful. If your brain, instead of your heart, pilots your emotions, there must be regrets. You *cannot* trust your brain. You *can* trust your heart. . . . You are a woman with a thousand little pockets in your being where you can tuck away little pains until tomorrow. A man hasn't got these pockets. His emotional system isn't quite as vast a labyrinth as yours. He is simpler, straighter than you are. [January 1954, p. 36]

Today one finds much more of a balance in magazine articles. Both husband and wife are shown to participate in making a marriage work. Both share in sexuality, birth control and pleasuring. Roles and expectations are evolving. We appreciate that men and women are different, but remain convinced that there exist many more significant similarities than divergences.

Some people want to go back to the good old days; we don't. Seventy years ago women couldn't vote. Margaret Sanger was arrested for urging women to practice birth control, even as thousands died as a result of unwanted pregnancies. The patriarchal family, which often preoccupied itself with a grim struggle for survival, enslaved women. It reduced the female to a breeder and caretaker of children, a servant to her spouse, a cleaning lady and at times a victim of the labor market. Children, in reacting to the impossible demands of being seen and not heard, not to mention slave-style child employment, often ran away from home or married early, thus effecting what they perceived as an escape. The father's dominance more often than not created a wall between him and the rest of his family.

Today, about two thirds of American families live "comfortably." Women need no longer produce more children than they want. Children express their own opinions and have the right to be educated and protected. At last men can relax, if they choose to break old sexist taboos.

THE FATHER'S ROLE

In egalitarian marriages, everyone benefits. The woman who is a full-time housekeeper and mother welcomes her husband's contribution and does not feel threatened or consider her husband less of a man for helping out. The partners are independently dependent and *choose* to support each other freely. The children in such marriages grow up in an atmosphere of community spirit and perceive the relationship of their parents as something deeply caring and whole. The open affection and communication between such parents will be the children's model for their own future relationships. The children themselves will be more likely to pitch in and help if they see that running a household is not a burden to be tossed single-handedly onto their mother's shoulders.

The fullest understanding of women's roles develops in those men who choose for a time to be "househusbands." That is, they work in the home and assume the primary responsibility for domestic and child-rearing tasks. Not a large number of men have pursued this option, but enough have to demonstrate the radical changes in how husbands' and wives' roles are perceived.

The concept of "maternal instinct" has long been held as the rationale for women assuming the major portion of child rearing and care. Yet research and countless testimonials from mothers, as well as men who partake in the care of their children, illustrates that there is no biological or gender-based parenting instinct. Except for breast-feeding, men and women are equally capable of raising and caring for a child.

Fathers can be involved with their infant's care from the beginning, by participating in prepared-childbirth classes and being present at the delivery of the child. By their diapering, feeding and holding the infant, an early, primal bond is formed. The child becomes familiar with the father's scent and voice, the feel of his hands and body, the texture of his clothing, all of which are different from the mother's manner of handling the baby. The father's involvement helps the child accept and learn a variety of stimuli and appreciate the role of a father's love. As the child develops and matures, the father will continue to enjoy a natural, spontaneous basis for relating to the child. Fathers who shun such early involvement, waiting perhaps for the child's first words, first day at school or even graduation, generally find it difficult to establish close ties.

The average father was until recently a passive figure in the home environment: it has been estimated that he spent *twenty-five minutes a week* in direct one-to-one interaction with his son or daughter. Many children report that they grew up hardly knowing their fathers. Despite the very real demands of providing for his family, fathers should set aside a certain amount of time each day to be spent with each child. Just fifteen minutes a day alone, especially with younger children, can have a big impact on their lifelong relationships. Teenagers might prefer longer blocks of time on a less regular basis. Taking turns allowing the child to plan how the time is to be spent will complement the activities planned by the father. The father's influence in teaching, disciplining and playing with the child will supplement and enhance the mother's role. Fathers can join their children in a wide range of experiences, from chess and checkers, political discussions and talks of sports, friends, school, to spontaneous unstructured fun.

Fathers can take their children out for a game of catch or stickball in the backyard or the local park, interest them in other sports and hobbies they enjoy or show them that household tasks when shared can be fun. Often fathers try to involve their children in some aspect of their career, perhaps starting early to groom the child for entry into the family business. Whatever the case, fathers should not expect that their children will automatically adopt the father's interests or want someday to walk in the father's footsteps. Beyond encouragement and suggestions, fathers should be particularly sensitive to the child's own interests and aspirations.

It is vital for children to learn that fathers, indeed males, can be affectionate, display warmth, share their feelings and thoughts, and be loving and giving. The father can be a role model and confidant without relinquishing his disciplinary function.

During the course of these exchanges, fathers should create opportunities to discuss issues pertaining to family life, sex education and other areas of interest to the child. It is vital for fathers not to relegate this responsibility to their wives. Children benefit from *both* parents' perspectives, and mothers usually resent the father's lack of involvement. Despite their own sexist upbringings, fathers need not convey those same messages to their children. Comments such as "Act like a man," "That's the way women are" and "Girls don't do things like that" are not helpful to the child. Fathers can also create handicaps for their daughters by sheltering them while at the same time encouraging their sons to explore the environment. Fathers have a great opportunity, however, to help children of both sexes develop their special capabilities and understand their sexuality in positive, self-affirming ways.

The quality of love and caring between the parents is the most significant aspect of children's sexuality education. Yet fathers can create numerous other opportunities for teachable moments in the education of their children. Before the age of five, many fathers shower with their children or bathe them, using the occasions to discuss issues related to physical maturation and instill positive feelings about one's body. Many parents enjoy having their children join them in bed on weekend mornings for some playful wrestling and conversation. Around the age of five, most children develop their own sense of privacy and will want to curtail these activities.

It is important for fathers to understand that silence on issues of human sexuality teaches children as much as openness does—but in a negative way. Fathers can get discussions going by talking about their childhood and adolescent feelings and experiences. What better way for a child to learn than to hear of his or her father's first experiences in love? Without revealing the sexual details of his life, a father can transmit the message that sexual feelings cross all generation gaps and enter into all lifestyles and age groups.

Around the time the child enters school, fathers often begin to fear displays of affection with both their sons and their daughters. They fear that the son will mature to be effeminate or homosexual; they worry lest their daughter may develop an erotic sexual attraction for the father as the male figure in her life. Thus, the children are left bewildered and hurt at their father's withdrawal of affection, and they attribute it to something they (the child) did wrong. After a while, they may come to see it as simply being the way Dad is. The father's fears of negatively influencing the sexual development of his children are unfounded. There is no evidence to support the theory that sons with affectionate fathers become homosexuals, or that daughters will compete with the mother for the father's sexual attentions. Some girls love to flirt and play seductive games with their fathers, which is simply a way of affirming their attractiveness. Boys who enjoy their father's affections will, if anything, grow up to be less inhibited about themselves, their bodies and their relationships with others of both sexes.

The fear of expressing warmth and physical attentions to children may also derive from the father's fear of becoming sensually or sexually stimulated. It is not uncommon to feel somewhat aroused by the wrestling and close body contact with one's children. Fathers are apt to experience warm, mildly erotic feelings similar to the ones their wives encounter when breastfeeding or holding children. These interchanges help teach children to be sensual and loving when they grow up. Fathers who feel guilty or embarrassed about those feelings mistakenly think it preferable to withhold physical intimacies from children. Fathers can relax and enjoy the love of their children. (It goes without saying that translating those erotic feelings into specifically sexual behavior is never warranted.)

Dire predictions abound regarding the current liberation movement. According to them, we can look forward to emasculated husbands, children confused over their gender identity and sexual orientation, and women more unhappy than ever once deprived of their historic homemaker role. One need only visit a home where opportunities are equal to see that these predictions are not valid. Fathers especially report that a huge weight has been lifted from their shoulders once they are freed of the compulsion to wear a Great Stone Face in order to be macho.

Let's examine that term "macho" and what it has come to represent. In English, it signifies a man who is a sexual bully, who sees women as objects for his sexual satisfaction, and who goes out drinking or fighting to prove his masculinity. A macho man is domineering, insensitive and tough. In Spanish, however, the language the term derived from, it has very different connotations. Men of all nationalities—including the Latin—have twisted the meaning around. The term originally described a man who was strong and able to handle the problems of life, poverty and suffering. *Macho* was often used in a family context for men who took the responsibility of being good fathers and husbands, who were respectful of others, and who treated their women and children with love and respect. Above all, the word originally meant a sense of man's own dignity.

GRANDPARENTS

If there is one thing to lament about the passing of the traditional family, it is the abandonment of old people to nursing homes and retirement "ghettos." Yet, as Kornhaber and Woodward write in their poignant book *Grandparents/Grandchildren: The Vital Connection*, "Every time a child is born, a grandparent is born too." We share their belief that grandparents' ongoing interaction with families is a vital part of family life. In fact, many family therapists, Jay Haley, Carl Whitaker and Salvador Minuchin among them, actively include grandparents in family therapy sessions. This multigenerational model of family functioning highlights the significance of maintaining close ties among all members.

As secondary caretakers of their children's children, grandparents have a wealth of love and experience to offer. Their main consideration is to be responsive to the parents' rules and guidelines, and not to impinge on their authority. Grandparents may get into trouble when they convey certain values and attitudes the parents do not share, or even feed the children foods the parents don't approve of. It is important to respect the parents' own boundaries of strictness or permissiveness.

Many readers of this book probably have at least one grandparent still living, and their children almost certainly have one or more. Within families, grandparents represent the most visible roots of the family's heritage and bridge to the past. Grandparents have many stories to tell of what life was like during their own childhood and young-adult years. If they were born in a foreign land, they can convey fascinating information about the country and culture from which the family springs. Their experiences and memories of the past help to put the present into a better perspective and can do much to clarify how contemporary conditions and problems have developed. An enhanced understanding of the past, as Alex Haley has shown so vividly in his book *Roots,* can lead to a fuller appreciation of the present and may help to build a healthier family unit, marked by greater love and cohesiveness.

The book by Kornhaber and Woodward surveyed three hundred grandchildren and three hundred grandparents and discovered that only about 5 percent of them enjoy regular intimate interactions with one another. The study also indicates that about 80 percent of American grandchildren see their grandparents infrequently, if at all. It reveals that grandparents often refrain from relationships with their grandchildren for fear of "meddling" with the youngsters.

Children who are denied contacts with their grandparents become indifferent to them, with an exaggerated awareness of the distance between themselves and their oldest relatives. Though more grandparents are alive today than ever before, the authors report that a dismayingly small number of grandchildren benefit from what the older people have to offer—roles as care-taker, storyteller, family historian, mentor, wizard, confidant, negotiator between parent and child. Most important of all, perhaps, the grandchildren miss an opportunity to get some idea of what it is like to be old, and in a sense to start preparing for the later stages of their own lives. The self-esteem of all three generations is enhanced in families which respect one another's roles and contributions.

The traditional image of grandparents is that they tend to spoil and pamper children or impart overly rigid views concerning sexuality and life in general. They may say to their own children, "We raised you well and we know what's best"; some grandparents unfortunately alienate themselves by refusing to honor the parents' wishes. Imagine, for example, that Grandma particularly objects to a child's masturbation. While parents maintain their values in the midst of whatever conflict of opinion arises, Grandma can be told, "Oh, well, don't say anything to the child or scold him. You know how children are—you tell them not to do something and they do it twice as much." This may sound a bit condescending, but it works.

While some sexual issues, and our openness to talking about them, have changed dramatically since today's grandparents were young, human sexuality itself has changed little, if at all. Today's elderly have struggled with the same problems of faith, morals, social outlook and search for meaning and purpose as today's younger generations.

If some old people seem close-minded on the subject of sexuality, it is not only because they were raised in more puritanical times. Even today, societal prejudices hold that to be old is to be sexless. Unlike tribal or rural societies, our modern urban society gives lip service to the values of maturity while, at the same time, placing the strongest possible emphasis on the joys of youth. Unfortunately, many older people accept the sexless bed that society has laid for them. Not wanting to be ridiculed or feel society's disapproval, many suppress their sexual desires for fear that they might be tagged as "abnormal" or "oversexed" by their friends, neighbors and children.

An older man with buoyant sexual drives is often referred to as a "dirty old man" or a lecher. Perhaps some are, but they hardly approach the proportion of lechers found among younger people. Yet, years ago, Kinsey discovered that many older people do remain sexually active, though this fact appears to be one of society's best-kept secrets.

Our position is that sexuality is common to all age groups. People of all ages need both intimacy and emotional contacts. Older people can continue to enjoy physical relationships throughout their entire life span. One pervasive myth many old people must confront is that sexual intercourse is the only form of sexual activity. It is forgotten that touching, holding, genital play and other intimate expressions all constitute human sexuality. Perhaps some older persons place less emphasis on erection, lubrication or orgasm in favor of other sexual expressions, but that hardly makes them less sexual. Furthermore, research indicates that sexual inability in older individuals is not primarily a function of physiological factors. Instead, psychological and social forces related to aging appear much more significant.

The policies and attitudes which younger people establish today toward older citizens will affect themselves tomorrow. In this sense, raising a sexually conservative child means imparting respect for all stages of the life span, including one's own old age. The high levels of self-acceptance which parents help their children develop will generally remain with the child into adulthood and the later years.

*   *   *

For the first time in history, we are beginning to notice glimmerings of the excitement, the joy and the power of family life, based fundamentally on the fact that couples marry not for political or economic reasons, not for escape, sex or pregnancy, but because they love each other. Women and men respect each other and have children because they want them. They spend time having fun together. Many are beginning to discover that religion need be neither a burden nor a farce, but an affirmation of the spirit that brings comfort, joy and relaxation to a hectic, complex life.

We reserve our highest praise for authentic pro-family people: millions of couples who remain married, who still care for each other and who are not ashamed to acknowledge it; millions of children who enjoy the fact that their parents are basically nice people; families who respect one another's ideas, impulses and idiosyncrasies; families who, even if split by divorce or untimely death, find in such events an opportunity for growth and a re-affirmation of values. Children who grow up in such families develop good self-esteem and tend to adopt their parents' values as their own.

It's up to you—the parents—to prepare today's youth for tomorrow's family.

CHAPTER THIRTEEN

The Case for a Moral Sex Education

F irst we must make the case for a moral education in the public schools. "Our liberal democratic heritage expressed in the American constitutional framework of secular limited government is our strongest bulwark for personal liberty and human rights," says Edward L. Ericson, in *American Freedom and The Radical Right*. "True moral democracy . . . is always a morality of diversity, liberty and civil tolerance."

As Aristotle suggested, people do not naturally grow up to be morally excellent. They become so only as a result of a lifelong personal and community effort.

Human beings are not necessarily born with a capacity for behaving democratically or altruistically. One reason why moral development is a lifelong process has to do with the complexity of almost any human issue. Moral development takes place within a community of persons; any individual's sense of right and wrong develops in interaction with others. For one individual to impose dogmatically his or her point of view on another would interfere with moral development and individual liberty.

There is a vast difference between being moral and being moralistic. Moralistic stances leave little room for dissent and dialogue. For example, a teacher could state that it is a health hazard for young people to smoke. This is a statement of a moral position. It would be moralistic for the teacher to declare, "It is a sin to smoke." Moralistic statements clearly are inappropriate for public schools, but might be appropriate for parochial schools, where dogma can be taught.

The tension between one person's liberty and another's is a moral issue. Put another way, a central moral dilemma is, how can I exercise my individual liberty without harming another person or myself? Or, how can I exercise my individual liberty and enhance the growth of another?

Young people need to understand these complex issues. They need to learn how to apply moral principles to situations in their own lives. The community—that is, parents, teachers and clergy—have the responsibility to help young people. If principles are imposed with no room for discussion and working through, then the possibility of developing into a morally excellent person is prematurely foreclosed.

If, at its heart, education is moral education, then we have to face the fact that values will be part of the process. Education cannot be conducted in a value-free context.

In social studies, for example, the teacher doesn't say, "All forms of government are equally good. Choose one." The teacher explains that democracy is what the founding American fathers thought was best. Democracy, in their understanding, offers the maximum benefits to the most people and protects them from exploitation. The notion of democracy, then, is value-laden. The Constitution guarantees the right to life, liberty and the pursuit of happiness. Laws protect us from persons who interfere with these rights.

Moral education would foster the basic values embodied in the Bill of Rights. Since America is a democratic society, and public schools are committed to these values, moral education is logical and appropriate for American society. The basic principle of a moral education is the democratic principle of human equality. In practice, it is difficult to apply, but it provides a goal toward which educators can help students strive.

The values to be taught, then, are the values of a democratic society. They are not static in some of their applications: the Constitution is amended from time to time. The essence of these values, however, is considered universal and unchanging over time. The concept of community standards, so often applied to controversies on the local level in regard to racial or sexual matters, needs to be examined carefully when designing a moral education. Racist attitudes did, and in some ways still do, reflect community standards in sections of our country. Yet it is wrong to teach racism in the schools.

In moral education, however, we teach the highest aspirations of our society, no matter what is manifested in isolated locales or in the pronouncements of extremist groups. Equality of the sexes, dignity and respect for all human beings regardless of their race, religion, sexual orientation or country of origin all stem from the fundamental democratic premise of equality.

In this context, all controversial issues can be discussed, even such volatile issues as abortion and masturbation. But if you're going to deal with a controversial issue, you must, fairly and rationally, present a range of points of view that exist on the matter. Even in this setting, however, one cannot tell lies, and one must present the range of opinion in a rational manner in keeping with a scientific perspective.

Proselytizing in the public schools violates our constitutional rights and liberties. In this country we are firmly committed to separation of church and state. Of course we endorse a value-laden, moral education, but whose values? Ours. The moral aspirations of the democratic society in which we live. We are opposed to racism, sexism and the double standard. We favor equal opportunities for men and women. We are not clarifying our values with regard to rape, we're opposed to rape and sexual exploitation of children.

It's not difficult to make a distinction between using good judgment and being judgmental. We are, after all, a democratic society, dedicated to diversity of opinion and religious beliefs. This doesn't mean we're not clear about what we want to accomplish in terms of justice without being influenced by race, religion and gender. We are not dumb; we know that life is not fair, but our laws should be.

Although American society subscribes to the principle of equality, in practice the poor, blacks, the disabled, women and children are often exceptions. There are many other ways to damage the dignity of others, coercion being one. Intimidation can involve physical aggression or threats, or it can play upon another person's sense of self. The classic words of coercion in male–female relationships are, "You would if you loved me." Exposure to moral education mitigates against exploitation in the guise of seduction and demonstrates how moral development would be enhanced by teaching a full range of these ideas.

Some school systems are now teaching moral values. The Salt Lake City School District, for example, has introduced moral education into its curriculum. Some of their basic principles illustrate how democratic values can be an explicit part of the curriculum with time set aside for student discussion. Here are some of the principles:

1. Each individual has dignity and worth.
2. A free society requires respect for all persons, property, and principles.
3. Each person is responsible for his or her own actions.
4. Each individual has a responsibility to the group as well as to the total society.

Mary S. Calderone and Eric Johnson (*The Family Book About Sexuality*), both preoccupied with the moral dimensions of sexuality, developed a perspective that is useful for our purpose. They suggest that the following six values should be acceptable in our American democracy.

1. The value of information.
2. The value of responsibility.
3. The value of control.
4. The value of consideration.
5. The value of each individual person.
6. The value of communication.

We firmly endorse the position approved by the Values Education Commission of the Maryland State Department of Education, July 30, 1979:

> . . . the Commission takes the view that the public schools are appropriate, indeed necessary, institutions in a democratic society for defining and encouraging character and citizenship

values. The schools cannot supplant the role played by the family and religion in values education, but they can reinforce positive attitudes and behavior and counteract negative influences on the students.

The Commission recognizes that responsible personal and citizenship behavior can be encouraged by the entire public school experience as well as by special efforts within the curriculum to deal with the rights and duties of citizens in a democracy.

CHARACTER OBJECTIVES

1. Personal integrity and honesty rooted in respect for the truth, intellectual curiosity, and love of learning.
2. A sense of duty to self, family, school and community.
3. Self-esteem rooted in the recognition of one's potential.
4. Respect for the rights of all persons regardless of their race, religion, sex, age, physical condition, or mental state.
5. A recognition of the right of others to hold and express differing views, combined with the capacity to make discriminating judgments among competing opinions.
6. A sense of justice, rectitude, fair play and a commitment to them.
7. A disposition of understanding, sympathy, concern and compassion for others.
8. A sense of discipline and pride in one's work; respect for the achievements of others.
9. Respect for one's property and the property of others, including public property.
10. Courage to express one's convictions.

CITIZENSHIP OBJECTIVES

1. Patriotism: love, respect and loyalty to the United States of America and the willingness to correct its imperfections by legal means.
2. An understanding of the rights and obligations of a citizen in a democratic society.
3. An understanding of other societies in a world which do not enjoy the rights and privileges of a democratic government.
4. Respect for the U.S. Constitution, the rule of law and the

right of every citizen to enjoy equality under the law. An understanding of the Bill of Rights and a recognition that all rights are limited by other rights and by obligations. Respect for legitimate authority at the local, state and federal levels.

5. Allegiance to the concept of democratic government as opposed to totalitarian rule. A recognition that government is limited by the separation of powers and by the countervailing role of other institutions in a pluralistic society—principally the family, religion, the school and the private sector of the economy.

6. Recognition of the need for an independent court system to protect the rights of all citizens.

7. An acceptance of all citizenship responsibilities at the local, state and national levels and a commitment to preserve and defend the United States and its democratic institutions.

John Dewey suggested in the late 1800s that school should focus less on what to do and more on "how to decide what to do."

Dewey opposed moral instructions which relied heavily on oaths, creeds, codes, prayers and extrinsic rewards. In order to facilitate moral development, Dewey suggested, schools should provide opportunities in cooperation, self-direction and leadership rather than conformity, passivity and blind submission to authority.

Eighty-three percent of Americans favor sex education in the schools, according to a 1983 Roper poll. Yet less than 10 percent of American schoolchildren are exposed to anything approaching a good sex education. All you need is three or four opponents in almost any community and the sex education program is finished, because school boards are overly responsive to these extremists. Fortunately, after a long, hard struggle this did not turn out to be the fate in New Jersey, where sex education is now mandated.* Sex education opponents in New Jersey still, however, object to school administrators teaching values to their students. Administrators respond that they don't teach values,

* One of only two states in the country as of 1986.

they merely clarify them. Nobody wants people without values teaching our children. A sex education without values is *valueless*.

Opponents of sex education want you to believe that if you tell kids about sex they'll do it. Yet all our research reveals that young people who are knowledgeable about their sexuality are more likely to delay their first sexual experience. Knowledge isn't harmful. If there is one message to spread far and wide, it's that knowledge is not harmful. Virtually all opposition in this country to sex education is based on the supposition that knowledge is harmful.

Let me conclude by telling you a true story that represents the value of values. A young college student came to me absolutely in despair and said, "Listen, my boyfriend and I took your course and we plan to get married, but our marriage is threatened because he wants to have sex before marriage and I don't. I don't care if I'm the last virgin. I want to be a virgin on my wedding night. We had such a fight that we decided to compromise. We will leave it up to Dr. Gordon to decide."

Now, if I were a modern psychologist I would say, "Listen, I can't tell you what to do, you need therapy. At the end I still won't be able to tell you what to do, because I can't impose my values on you. You'll develop a little insight and you'll figure out what to do." I didn't say that. I said, "Listen, if you have sex with him under those circumstances, you're stupid." She was thrilled, but wanted to know what she should tell him. I said to tell him that if he really loved her he wouldn't put this kind of pressure on her. She said, "Oh my God, that never occurred to me." (A college senior yet.) She went home to talk to her boyfriend. A half hour later she called me and said, "I told him." What did he say? "He said you have a point."

APPENDIX A

Recommended Reading for Parents and Children Who Want to Know More
A SELECTED LIST

For Parents of Young Children

Aho, J. J., and J. Petras. *Learning About Sex: A Guide for Children and Their Parents.* New York: Holt, Rinehart and Winston, 1978.

Bernstein, A. *The Flight of the Stork.* New York: Delacorte, 1978.

Briggs, D. C. *Your Child's Self-Esteem.* New York: Dolphin Books, 1975.

Calderone, M. S., and E. W. Johnson. *The Family Book About Sexuality.* New York: Lippincott & Crowell, 1980. Available in paperback.

———, and J. W. Ramey. *Talking with Your Child About Sex: Questions and Answers for Children from Birth to Puberty.* New York: Random House, 1982.

Gitchel, S., and L. Foster. *Let's Talk About S-E-X: A Read and Discuss Guide for People 9–12 and Their Parents.* Available from Planned Parenthood of Fresno, California.

Gochros, J. *What to Say After You Clear Your Throat: A Parents' Guide to Sex Education.* Kailua, HI: Press Pacifica, 1980.

Gordon, S., and I. R. Dickman. *Sex Education: The Parent's Role* (Pamphlet No. 549). New York: Public Affairs Committee, 1977.

Lerrigo, M., and H. Southard. *Parents' Responsibility,* revised edition. American Medical Association, 1976.

Lyman, M. *Sex Education at Home: A Guide for Parents.* Syracuse, NY: Planned Parenthood, 1974.

Pogrebin, L. *Growing Up Free: Raising Your Child in the '80s.* New York: McGraw-Hill, 1980.

Ross, S. S. *What Is Sex Education All About? A Guide for Parents.* Chicago: Adams Press, 1979.

Scanzoni, L. D. *Sex Is a Parent Affair: A Responsible Guide for Teaching Your Children About Sex.* New York: Bantam Books, 1982.

Warren, J. *Parents Ask About Sex Education* (pamphlet). Available from Ed-U Press, P.O. Box 583, Fayetteville, NY 13066.

For Parents of Teenagers

Dickman, I. R. *Teenage Pregnancy: What Can Be Done?* (Pamphlet No. 594). New York: Public Affairs Committee, 1981.

Landers, A. *High School Sex and How to Deal with It: A Guide for Teens and Their Parents.* See her column for ordering information.

Le Shan, E. J. *Sex and Your Teenager: A Guide for Parents.* New York: McKay, 1969.

Lewis, R., and M. E. Lewis. *The Parents' Guide to Teenage Sex and Pregnancy.* New York: St. Martin's Press, 1980.

Oettinger, K. B., with E. C. Mooney. *Not My Daughter: Facing Up to Adolescent Pregnancy.* Englewood Cliffs, NJ: Prentice-Hall, 1979.

For Children Under Seven

Andry, A. C., and S. Schepp. *How Babies Are Made.* New York: Time-Life Books, 1968.

Gordon, S., and J. Gordon. *Did the Sun Shine Before You Were Born?*, 2nd edition. Fayetteville, NY: Ed-U Press, 1979.

Levine, M. I., and J. Seligmann. *A Baby Is Born.* New York: Golden Press, 1978.

Stein, S. *Making Babies: An Open Family Book.* New York: Walker, 1974.

Waxman, S. *A Child's Introduction to Sexuality.* Los Angeles, CA: Panjandrum Books, 1979.

For Children from About Seven to Eleven

Gordon, S. *Girls Are Girls and Boys Are Boys—So What's the Difference?*, 2nd edition. Fayetteville, NY: Ed-U Press, 1979.

Gruenberg, S. M. *The Wonderful Story of How You Were Born.* New York: Doubleday, 1973.

Nilsson, L. *How Was I Born?* New York: Delacorte, 1975.

Rushnell, E. E. *My Mom's Having a Baby.* New York: Grosset & Dunlap, 1978.

For Preteens

Gardner-Loulan, J., B. Lopez, and M. Quackenbush. *Period.* San Francisco: Volcano Press, 1979.

Johnson, C. B., and E. W. Johnson. *Love and Sex and Growing Up.* New York: Bantam Books, 1979.

Mayle, P. *What's Happening to Me?* Secaucus, NJ: Lyle Stuart, 1975.

For Teenagers Who Don't Like to Read Much

Gordon, S. *You Would If You Loved Me.* New York: Bantam Books, 1978.

————. *Facts About Sex for Today's Youth,* 3rd edition. Fayetteville, NY: Ed-U Press, 1983.

————. *Facts About STD,* 2nd edition. Fayetteville, NY: Ed-U Press, 1983.

Johnson, E. W. *Love and Sex in Plain Language.* New York: Bantam Books, 1974.

For Both Teenagers Who Don't Like to Read Much and Those Who Do

Gordon, S. *The Teenage Survival Book.* New York: Times Books, Revised 1985.

Hettlinger, R. *Growing Up with Sex.* New York: Continuum, 1980.

For Young Adults (About Sixteen and Up)

Bell, R. *Changing Bodies, Changing Lives.* New York: Random House, 1980.

Comfort, A., and J. Comfort. *The Facts of Love: Living, Loving and Growing Up.* New York: Crown, 1980.

Eagan, A. B. *Why Am I So Miserable If These Are the Best Years of My Life?* New York: Avon, 1979.

Gordon, S. *The New You.* New York: Bantam Books, 1979.

————, and M. Wollin. *Parenting: A Guide for Young People,* revised edition. New York: Sadlier, 1983.

Hamilton, E. *Sex with Love: A Guide for Young People.* Boston: Beacon Press, 1978.

Hettlinger, R. *Your Sexual Freedom. Letters to Students.* New York: Continuum, 1982.

Jampolsky, G. *Love Is Letting Go of Fear.* New York: Bantam Books, 1980.

Kelly, G. F. *Learning About Sex: A Contemporary Guide for Young Adults.* Woodbury, NY: Barron's Educational Services, 1976.

Lieberman, E. J., and E. Peck. *Sex and Birth Control: A Guide for the Young.* New York: Harper & Row, 1981. Available in paperback.

McCoy, K. *The Teenage Body Book.* New York: Wallaby, 1982.

Riker, A. P., and C. Riker. *Finding My Way.* Peoria, IL: Charles A. Bennett Co., 1979.

Rikert, R. *Sexuality and Dating.* Winona, MN: St. Mary's Press, 1981.

Shedd, C. *How to Know If You're Really in Love.* Kansas City, KS: Sheed, Andrews & McNeal, 1978.

Short, R. E. *Sex, Love or Infatuation: How Can I Really Know?* Minneapolis: Augsburg Publishing House, 1978.

Homosexuality

Fairchild, B., and N. Hayward. *Now That You Know: What Every Parent Should Know About Homosexuality.* New York: Harcourt Brace Jovanovich, 1979.

Hobson, L. Z. *Consenting Adult.* New York: Warner Books, 1976. Fiction based on real-life occurrence.

McNaught, B. *A Disturbed Peace.* Washington: Dignity, Inc., 1981. Available from Ed-U Press, P.O. Box 583, Fayetteville, NY 13066.

McNeill, J. J. *The Church and the Homosexual.* New York: Pocket Books, 1976.

Silverstein, C. *A Family Matter.* New York: McGraw-Hill, 1977.

Religion and Sexuality

Borowitz, E. B. *Choosing a Sex Ethic: A Jewish Inquiry.* New York: Schocken Books, 1969.

Clapp, S., S. Brownfield, and J. Seibert. *A Christian View of Youth and Sexuality.* Sidell, IL: C-4 Resources, P.O. Box 27, Sidell, IL 61876.

Gittelsohn, R. *Love, Sex and Marriage: A Jewish View.* New York: Union of American Hebrew Congregations, 1980.

Gordis, R. *Love and Sex: A Modern Jewish Perspective.* New York: Farrar, Straus and Giroux, 1978.

Keane, P. S. *Sexual Morality: A Catholic Perspective.* New York: Paulist Press, 1977.

Koznik, A., et al. *Human Sexuality: New Directions in American Catholic Thought.* New York: Paulist Press, 1977.

National Committee for Human Sexuality Education, United States Catholic Conference. *Education in Human Sexuality for Christians.* Washington: 1981.

Nelson, J. B. *Embodiment: An Approach to Sexuality and Christian Theology.* Minneapolis: Augsburg Publishing House, 1978.

Smedes, L. B. *Sex for Christians.* Grand Rapids, MI: William B. Eerdmans, 1976.

Taylor, J. J., ed. *Sex: Thoughts for Contemporary Christians.* New York: Doubleday, 1972.

Disabilities

Ayrault, E. W. *Sex, Love and the Physically Handicapped.* New York: Continuum, 1981.

Blum, G., and B. Blum. *Feeling Good About Yourself.* 1981. Available from Feeling Good Associates, 507 Palma Way, Mill Valley, CA 94941.

Buscaglia, L., ed. *The Disabled and Their Parents*, new edition. Thorofare, NJ: Charles B. Slack, 1983.

Cornelius, D. A., et al. *Who Cares? A Handbook on Sex Education and Counseling Services for Disabled People*, 2nd edition. Baltimore, MD: University Park Press, 1982.

Dickman, I. R. *Sex Education for Disabled Persons* (Pamphlet No. 531). New York: Public Affairs Committee, 1975.

Johnson, W. R., and W. Kempton. *Sex Education and Counseling of Special Groups: The Mentally and Physically Handicapped, Ill and Elderly*, 2nd edition. Springfield, IL: Charles C. Thomas, 1980.

Kempton, W., et al. *Love, Sex and Birth Control for the Mentally Retarded: A Guide for Parents.* Available from Ed-U Press, P.O. Box 583, Fayetteville, NY 13066.

McKee, L., and V. Blacklidge. *Sexuality and Socialization. A Book for Parents of People with Mental Handicaps.* 1981. Available from Ed-U Press, P.O. Box 583, Fayetteville, NY 13066.

Robinault, I. P. *Sex, Society and the Disabled.* Hagerstown, MD: Harper & Row, 1978.

Single Parents

Adams, J. *Sex and the Single Parent.* New York: Coward, McCann and Geoghegan, 1978.

Di Giulio, R. C. *When You Are a Single Parent.* St. Meinrad, IN: Abbey Press, 1979.

Gatley, R., and D. Konlak. *Single Father's Handbook.* Garden City, NY: Doubleday Anchor, 1979.

Hope, K., and N. Young. *Momma: The Source Book for Single Mothers.* New York: New American Library, 1976.

Levine, J. A. *Who Will Raise the Children? New Options for Fathers (and Mothers).* New York: Bantam Books, 1977.

Weiss, R. S. *Going It Alone: The Family Life and Social Situation of the Single Parent.* New York: Basic Books, 1979.

Joint Custody

Galper, M. *Co-parenting: A Source Book for the Separated or Divorced Family.* Philadelphia: Running Press, 1978.

Stepfamilies: For Children and Adolescents

Bradley, B., and M. Cocca. *Where Do I Belong? A Kid's Guide to Stepfamilies.* Reading, MA: Addison-Wesley, 1982.

Burt, M. S., and R. B. Burt. *What's Special About Our Stepfamily?* New York: Doubleday, 1983.

Gardner, R. A. *The Boy's and Girl's Book About Stepfamilies.* New York: Bantam Books, 1982.

Stepparents

Berman, C. *Stepfamilies—A Growing Reality.* New York: Public Affairs Committee, 1982.

Capaldi, F., and B. McRae. *Stepfamilies: A Cooperative Responsibility; for Stepparents and Single Parents Considering Remarriage.* New York: New Viewpoints/Watts, 1979.

Craven, L. *Stepfamilies: New Patterns for Harmony.* New York: Simon and Schuster, 1982.

Visher, E., and J. Visher. *Stepfamilies.* Secaucus, NJ: Citadel Press, 1980.

Wald, E. *The Remarried Family: Challenge and Promise.* New York: Family Service Association of America, 1981.

Divorce

Barnett, P., et al. *Parenting Children of Divorce.* New York: Family Service Association of America, 1980.

Gardner, R. A. *The Parents' Book About Divorce.* New York: Bantam Books, 1978.

Jewett, E. L. *Helping Children Cope with Separation and Loss.* Cambridge, MA: Harvard Common Press, 1982.

Spilke, F. S. *What About the Children? A Divorced Parent's Handbook.* New York: Crown, 1979.

Divorce: For Children

Gardner, R. *The Boy's and Girl's Book About Divorce.* New York: Bantam Books, 1971.

Rofes, E., ed. *The Kid's Book of Divorce.* Brattleboro, VT: Lewis Publishing, 1981.

Sexual Molestation of Children

Armstrong, L. *Kiss Daddy Goodnight.* New York: Pocket Books, 1978.

Sanford, L. *The Silent Children: A Parent's Guide to the Prevention of Child Sexual Abuse.* New York: McGraw-Hill, 1981.

Pornography

The Report of the Commission on Obscenity and Pornography. New York: Bantam Books, 1970.

Birth Control

Hatcher, R. A., et al. *It's Your Choice: A Personal Guide to Birth Control Methods for Women—and Men Too.* New York: Irvington Publishers, 1982.

Sexual Sensitivity: Pleasure and Problem-Solving

Barbach, L. *For Each Other: Sharing Sexual Intimacy.* New York: Doubleday Anchor, 1982.

Gochros, H., and J. Fisher. *Treat Yourself to a Better Sex Life.* Englewood Cliffs, NJ: Prentice-Hall, 1980.

Greeley, A. *Sexual Intimacy.* Chicago: Thomas More Press, 1973.

Kennedy, E. C. *The New Sexuality: Myths, Fables and Hang-ups.* New York: Image Books (Doubleday), 1972.

Lehrman, N. *Masters and Johnson Explained.* Chicago: Playboy Press, 1974.

Masters, W. H., and V. E. Johnson, with R. J. Levin. *The Pleasure Bond: A New Look at Sexuality and Commitment.* Boston: Little, Brown, 1975.

McCarthy, B. W., M. Ryan and F. A. Johnson. *Sexual Awareness: A Practical Approach.* San Francisco: Boyd & Fraser, 1975.

Phillips, D., with R. Judd. *Sexual Confidence: Discovering the Joys of Intimacy.* Boston: Houghton Mifflin, 1980.

Shedd, C., and M. Shedd. *Celebration in the Bedroom.* Waco, TX: Word Books, 1981.

Zussman, L., and S. Zussman, with J. Brecher. *Getting Together: A Guide to Sexual Enrichment for Couples.* New York: William Morrow, 1979.

Men

Kelly, G. *Good Sex: The Healthy Man's Guide to Sexual Fulfillment.* New York: Harcourt Brace Jovanovich, 1979.

McCarthy, B. *What You (Still) Don't Know About Male Sexuality.* New York: Thomas Y. Crowell, 1977.

Zilbergeld, B. *Male Sexuality: A Guide to Sexual Fulfillment.* Boston: Little, Brown, 1978.

Women

Barbach, L. G. *For Yourself: The Fulfillment of Female Sexuality.* New York: Doubleday, 1975.

Cooke, C. W., and S. Divorkin. *The Ms. Guide to a Woman's Health.* New York: Doubleday Anchor, 1979.

Heinman, J., L. LoPiccolo and J. LoPiccolo. *Becoming Orgasmic: A Sexual Growth Program for Women.* Englewood Cliffs, NJ: Prentice-Hall, 1976.

Hite, S. *The Hite Report: A Nationwide Study of Female Sexuality.* New York: Macmillan, 1976.

Stewart, H. S., F. J. Guest, G. K. Stewart and R. A. Hatcher. *My Body, My Health: The Concerned Woman's Guide to Gynecology.* New York: John Wiley, 1979.

Sexually Transmitted Diseases

Corsaro, M., and C. Korzeniowsky. *STD: A Commonsense Guide.* New York: St. Martin's Press, 1980.

Lumiere, R., and S. Cook. *Healthy Sex . . . and Keeping It That Way.* New York: Simon and Schuster, 1983.

Wickett, W. H. *Herpes: Causes and Control.* New York: Pinnacle, 1982.

Sexuality and Aging

Butler, R., and M. L. Lewis. *Love and Sex After Sixty: A Guide for Men and Women for Their Later Years.* New York: Harper, 1977.

Comfort, A. *A Good Age.* New York: Crown, 1976.

Dickinson, P. A. *The Fires of Autumn: Sexual Activity in the Middle and Later Years.* New York: Sterling, 1977.

Sexuality Education in the Schools

Dickman, I. R. *Winning the Battle for Sex Education.* New York: SIECUS, revised 1986.

Gordon, S., and I. R. Dickman. *Schools and Parents: Partners in Sex Education* (Pamphlet No. 581). New York: Public Affairs Committee, 1979.

Jenkinson, E. B. *Censors in the Classroom.* New York: Avon, 1982.

Important Related Books of General Interest

Buscaglia, L. *Living, Loving and Learning.* Thorofare, NJ: Charles B. Slack, 1982.

Brown, L., ed. *Sex Education in the Eighties: The Challenge of Healthy Sexual Evolution.* New York: Plenum, 1981.

Carrera, M. *Sex: The Facts, the Acts and Your Feelings.* New York: Crown, 1981.

Ellis, A., and R. Harper. *A New Guide to Rational Living.* North Hollywood, CA: Wilshire Book Co., 1977.

Friedan, B. *The Second Stage.* New York: Summit Books, 1981.

Kennedy, E. *The Trouble Book.* New York: Cornerstone Library, reprinted 1977.

———. *On Being a Friend.* New York: Crossroad/Continuum, 1982.

Kornhaber, A., and K. Woodward. *Grandparents/Grandchildren:*

The Vital Connection. Garden City, NY: Doubleday Anchor, 1981.

Kushner, H. S. *When Bad Things Happen to Good People*. New York: Schocken, 1981.

Lasswell, M., and T. Lasswell. *Marriage and the Family*. Lexington, MA: D. C. Heath, 1982.

Mace, D. R. *Close Companions: The Marriage Enrichment Handbook*. New York: Crossroad/Continuum, 1982.

Maultsby, M. C., Jr. *Help Yourself to Happiness Through Rational Self-Counseling*. New York: Institute for Rational Living, 1975.

Peck, M. *The Road Less Traveled*. New York: Touchstone Books, 1978.

Roberts, E. J., ed. *Childhood Sexual Learning: The Unwritten Curriculum*. Cambridge, MA: Ballinger, 1980.

Salk, L. *My Father, My Son: Intimate Relationships*. New York: Putnam, 1982.

Schwarz, M., ed. *TV and Teens: Experts Look at the Issues*. Reading, MA: Addison-Wesley, 1982.

Shriver, Eunice Kennedy, ed. *A Community of Caring*. Washington, DC: The Joseph P. Kennedy Foundation, 1982.

Walker, Lenore. *The Battered Woman*. New York: Harper & Row, 1979.

New Books

Cassell, C. *Swept Away: Why Women Fear Their Own Sexuality*. New York: Bantam Books, 1985.

Dickman, I., with S. Gordon. *One Miracle at a Time: How to Get Help for a Disabled Child—Advice from Parents*. New York: Simon and Schuster, 1986.

Gordon, S. *When Living Hurts*. New York: Union of American Hebrew Congregations, 1985.

————, and J. Gordon. *A Better Safe Than Sorry Book: A Family Guide for Sexual Assault Prevention*. Fayetteville, N.Y.: Ed-U Press, revised 1986.

————, and C. W. Snyder. *Personal Issues in Human Sexuality*. Boston: Allyn & Bacon, 1986.

Sullivan, S. K., and M. A. Kawiak. *Parents Talk Love: The Catholic Family Handbook About Sexuality*. Mahwah, N.J.: Paulist Press, 1985.

Sources of Further Information

The American Medical Association
535 North Dearborn Street
Chicago, IL 60610

Center for Disease Control
(VD Control Division)
Building 1, Room 3051
1600 Clifton Road, N.E.
Atlanta, GA 30303

Center for Early Adolescence
Suite 223, Carr Mill Mall
Carrboro, NC 27510

The Family Life Section of your church or synagogue

Family Planning Program
Box 26069
80 Butler Street, S.E.
Atlanta, GA 30303

Herpes Resource Center
Box 100
Palo Alto, CA 94302

Center for Population Options
2031 Florida Avenue, N.W.
Washington, DC 20009

March of Dimes
1276 Mamaroneck Avenue
White Plains, NY 10605

National Clearinghouse for
Family Planning Information
P.O. Box 2225
Rockville, MD 20852

National Council of Churches
Commission on Marriage and
the Family
475 Riverside Drive
New York, NY 10027

National Education Association
1201 16th Street, N.W.
Washington, DC 20036

* The authors can be reached at this address.

National Family Life Education Network
1700 Mission Street, Suite 203
Santa Cruz, CA 95060

The National PTA
700 North Rush Street
Chicago, IL 60611

Planned Parenthood
810 Seventh Avenue
New York, NY 10019

Public Affairs Committee, Inc.
381 Park Avenue South
New York, NY 10016

For films:
Perennial Education, Inc.
477 Roger Williams
P.O. Box 855 Ravinia
Highland Park, IL 60035

For bibliographies and resources:
Ed-U Press
P.O. Box 583
Fayetteville, NY 13066

For families in special situations:
Child Welfare League of America
67 Irving Place
New York, NY 10003

For an excellent up-to-date pamphlet on sexually transmitted disease, send one dollar to:
American Foundation for the Prevention of
Venereal Disease, Inc.
799 Broadway, Suite 638
New York, NY 10003

For excellent bibliographies and newsletter:
SIECUS
80 Fifth Avenue
Suite 801-2
New York, NY 10011

For names of certified sexuality educators, counselors and therapists:
AASECT
Suite 700
1111 Fourteenth Street, N.W.
Washington, DC 20005

Index

*A Better Safe than Sorry Book:
A Family Guide for Sexual
Assault Prevention* (S. and
J. Gordon), 76
abortion, 64, 188
 in adolescence, 98–99
 timing of, 162
acne, 117
Acquaintance Rape, 152n
Acyclovir, 170
adolescence, 88–164
 abortion in, 98–99
 childbearing in, 92, 99, 147,
  162
 crushes in, 138
 cultural pressures in, 93–95,
  108
 homosexual experiences in,
  38, 131–38
 marriage in, 98
 motherhood in, 99
 orgasms in, 93, 154
 "performance anxiety" in,
  117
 pregnancy in, 43, 53, 89, 94–
  95, 96, 98, 103–4, 116, 147
 privacy in, 104, 186
 questions about, 112–43
 in Scandinavia, 63
 sexual intercourse in, 13, 43,
  53, 88–89, 91–92, 93, 102–
  103, 147
 sexual statistics on, 43, 88–
  89, 91–92, 99, 106, 111,
  147
 suicide in, 104
 vulnerability in, 95–97, 99
 see also boys; girls; teenagers
AIDS (Acquired Immune De-
  ficiency Syndrome), 166,
  173–74
alcohol, 14, 157–58
amebiasis, 173
*American Freedom and The
Radical Right* (Ericson),
 205
American Humanist Association, 62
antibiotics, 167, 172, 173
Aristotle, 205
attractiveness, 41, 117–18, 146,
  184, 187

baby talk, 45–46, 48
"bad reputation," 128–29, 147
Battered Women (Walker),
 193
Bernstein, Anne, 22
bestiality, 39
birth control, 48, 51, 54, 83, 97,
  148, 160–62, 172, 174,
  176, 195
 controversy over, 91, 92–93,
  115–16
 ignorance about, 43, 95
 in Scandinavia, 63
 as unromantic, 99, 124
births:
 abortion as alternative to, 98–
  99, 162
 out-of-wedlock, 14, 27, 92
 to teenage mothers, 92, 99
  147, 162
bisexuality, 32, 135
Blum, Gloria, 120
Blume, Judy, 124
books:
 for children, 17–18

books (*cont.*)
  for teenagers, 66, 104, 108,
    110, 124
boys:
  adolescent, 52, 91–95, 98–
    100, 102–3, 106, 115, 117–
    119, 123, 125, 129, 132–
    138, 148–50
  double standard and, 91–92,
    115
  father's relationship with,
    197–98
  masculinity worries of, 102
  nocturnal emission explained
    to, 79–80
  "performance anxiety" of,
    117, 157
  puberty of, 94
  sexual irresponsibility of, 98
    99, 111, 148
breasts, 37, 48–49

Calderone, Mary S., 208
Catcher in the Rye, The (Salin-
    ger), 34
celibacy, 37, 155
censorship, 16, 33–34, 62–63,
    140
Center for Disease Control,
    U.S., 166
chancre, 167–68
chancroid, 173
child abuse, 76–77, 99, 192–93
children, 68–87
  books for, 17–18
  disabled, 183–89
  elementary-school-age, ques-
    tions asked by, 82–85
  homosexual experiences of,
    38, 76
  in parents' bed, 75, 198
  preschool, 53
  preschool, questions asked by,
    80–82
  preteen, 79–80
  in single-parent families,
    179–83

  see also infancy
chlamydia, 166, 172
Citizens for Excellence in Edu-
    cation, 55
commercials, influence of, 14, 91
competence, development of
    feeling of, 25, 26
compulsive behavior, 40, 49,
    121, 129, 153, 156
condoms, 160, 174, 176
condyloma, 166
Consenting Adult (Hobson),
    137
conservatives, values of, 15–17,
    20
contraception, see birth control
corporal punishment, 16
crabs, 173, 178
curfews, 122

dating:
  early, 105, 121
  group vs. individual, 122, 187
  parents' questions about,
    121–31
  readiness for, 124
  steady, 127–28
  of "undesirables," 129
Deming, Alison, 115
Denmark, sexuality in, 63, 139
depression, 33, 146
Dewey, John, 210
*Did the Sun Shine Before You
    Were Born?* (S. and J.
    Gordon), 17
divorce, 13, 180–81, 192
Donahue, Phil, 91
double standard, in social ex-
    pectations, 41, 53, 61–62,
    64, 91–92, 98, 115, 129,
    154, 176, 193
dreams, 26, 39, 75, 142–43
  wet, 34, 79–80, 86–87
drugs, 14, 157–58

Educational Communications,
    102

ejaculation:
  first (onset of fertility), 94
  nocturnal, 34, 79–80, 86–87
  orgasm vs., 36, 157
  premature, 38, 41, 120, 157
Embodiment (Nelson), 28, 143
erection, 33, 119, 157
Ericson, Edward L., 205
Erikson, Erik, 23
exhibitionism, 39, 40

*Facts About Sex for Today's
    Youth* (S. Gordon), 66
families:
  future of, 191–203
  single-parent, 179–83, 192
  statistics on, 192
*Family Book About Sexuality,
    The* (Calderone and John-
    son), 208
fantasies, 32–33, 153
  guilt and, 32, 133
  homosexual, 39, 132, 133,136
  lust vs., 142–43
  masturbation and, 33
  about rape, 32, 142
fashion, influence of, 14, 33, 37,
    41, 93, 108
fathers, in egalitarian marriages,
    195–99
father–son discussions, 70
Federal Child Abuse Prevention
    and Treatment Act, 76–77
fetishism, 39, 40
films, influence of, 14, 90, 124
Ford, Betty, 103
Frankl, Viktor, 23
Freud, Sigmund, 36, 75, 135
Fromm, Erich, 23

Gabler, Mr. and Mrs., 62–63
genitals:
  infant play with, 72
  as "private" parts, 48–49, 51–
    52, 53, 78, 84
  size of, 36–37

giardiasis, 173
girls:
  adolescent, 42, 43, 51, 88–89,
    91–95, 98–100, 102–4,
    106, 116–18, 123, 125–26,
    128–29, 147–50, 154
  age of consent for, 98–99
  "aggressive," 125–26, 152
  black, 100
  desirability worries of, 98,
    102, 117–18, 126, 150
  double standard and, 61–62,
    98
  father's relationship with,
    197–98
  hygiene for, 171
  menstruation instruction for,
    19, 70, 79–80
  molestation of, 76, 134
  as mothers, 99
  "performance anxiety" of,
    117, 157
  pregnant, options for, 98–99
  promiscuous, 93, 128–29
  puberty of, 94
  runaway, 103–4
  suicidal, 104
  "tomboyish," 73
  vulnerability of, 99–100, 123,
    147
*Girls Are Girls and Boys Are
    Boys—So What's the Dif-
    ference?* (S. Gordon), 17,
    18
going steady, 127—28
Goldwater, Barry, 15
gonorrhea, 43, 163, 166, 168–
    169, 172, 176, 178
Gordon, Judith, 17, 191–92
Gordon, Sol, 17–18, 66, 69,
    149n, 191–92
grandparents, 199–202
Grandparents/Grandchildren
    (Kornhaber and Wood-
    ward), 199
Growing Up Free (Pogrebin),
    27

guilt, 93, 146, 153, 180, 189, 190, 192
  fantasies and, 32, 133
  about masturbation, 35, 49, 118, 156, 186
  mature vs. immature, 33
  molestation and, 52, 79

Hacker, Sylvia, 93
Haley, Jay, 199
handicaps, 96, 117, 183–89
Harris poll, 55
Henriksson, Benny, 25
hepatitis, 173, 178
herpes, 162–63, 166, 170–71, 173, 178
Hite, Shere, 30–31
homophobia, 38, 132, 133
homosexuality, 32, 38–39, 50–51, 71, 73, 95, 134–37, 158–60, 198
  in childhood and adolescence, 38, 76, 131–38
  defined, 135–36, 158, 160
  fantasies about, 39, 132, 133, 136
  latent, 133
  organizations for support of, 137
  statistics on, 135
  STDs and, 173–74
hostile-dependent relationship, 145
"househusbands," 195–96
Hunt, Morton, 181
hymen, 116, 151

impotence, 38, 41, 120
in vitro fertilization, 85
incest, 32, 76–77, 85
infancy:
  self-esteem in, 24
  sexuality in, 71–74
infant mortality, 99, 170, 171
inhibitions, 31, 120–21
IUD, 172

jealousy, 150
Jesus Christ, on lust, 142, 143
Johns Hopkins University, 42, 56, 88, 92
Johnson, Eric, 208

Keen, Sam, 20
Kinsey, Alfred, 135, 202
Kiss Daddy Goodnight (Armstrong), 76
Konopka, Gisela, 102

"latency" period, 75
LeHaye, Tim, 62
liberals, conservatives vs., 15
libraries, censorship and, 62–63
lice, pubic, 173
living together, 107
love:
  mature vs. immature, 105, 145
  possessiveness vs., 150
  questions about, 144–46
  sex vs., 19–20, 62, 99, 111, 123, 145, 147, 148
  withdrawal of, as punishment, 22
lust, 142–43

McClelland, David C., 20
"macho," 199
"making out," 127
marriage, 192
  in adolescence, 98
  egalitarian, 194–99
  mature, characteristics of, 30
  readiness for, 50–51, 187–88
masochism, 39
masturbation, 32, 34–35, 87, 118–21, 156, 157
  as alternative to sexual intercourse, 38, 100–101
  compulsive, 40, 49, 121, 156
  fantasy and, 33
  guilt about, 35, 49, 118, 156, 186
  punishment for, 118

synonyms for, 119–20
"maternal instinct," 196
media:
  influence of, 14, 19–20, 90–
    91, 96, 124
  overreaction of, 96, 103
men:
  desire in, 154
  homophobic, 38
  insecurity of, 36, 41, 193
  masturbation by, 34, 120
  nocturnal emission of, 34
  orgasms of, 36
menstruation, 42, 83, 86, 94,
    95, 162
  conversations about, 19, 70,
    79–80, 183
Miklowitz, Gloria D., 124
Minuchin, Salvador, 199
"missionary position," 35
molestation, 51–52, 76–79
  guilt and, 52, 79
  statistics on, 76, 78, 134
moral behavior, 27–28
mother–daughter discussions,
    19, 70
movies, influence of, 14, 90, 124
*My Mother Said . . . The Way
    Young People Learned
    About Sex and Birth Con-
    trol* (Farrell), 67

National Center for Health Sta-
    tistics, 13–14
National Center on Child
    Abuse and Neglect, 76–77
National Gay Task Force, 137
necrophilia, 39
New York Times, 115–16
NGU (nongonococcal urethri-
    tis), 166, 169–70, 172, 178
nightmares, 26, 75
nocturnal emission, 34, 79–80,
    86–87
Nozick, Robert, 23
nudity, 48, 49, 53

obscene language, 49
orgasm:
  in adolescence, 93, 154
  anxiety about, 117
  dreams as cause of, 34, 86–87
  ejaculation vs., 36, 157
  female, 34, 35–36, 41, 87, 93,
    117, 154–55, 156
  learning about, 119–20, 155
  male, 36, 87, 93, 157
  psychological nature of, 36
  sexuality vs., 20
  simultaneous, 35
ovulation, 162

parental conflict, 112–13
parent–child discussions, 42–54
  baby talk in, 45–46, 48
  father–son, 70
  importance of, 33, 68–69, 92
  inhibitions in, 31, 45
  initiation of, 28, 52, 104
  mother–daughter, 19, 70
  privacy vs., 26, 75, 104, 114,
    180
  statistics on, 19
  truthfulness important in,
    123, 180
parents, advice to, 130–31
Parents Anonymous, 78
PARENTS FLAG (Parents
    and Friends of Lesbians
    and Gays), 137
parents' rights, 130, 189
parties, adult supervision of,
    122, 124
Peck, M. Scott, 21
peer groups:
  homophobic, 132, 133
  pressure exerted by, 14, 15,
    122, 147, 151
pelvic inflammatory disease
    (PID), 172, 176
penis, size of, 36, 155
penis envy, 36
"performance anxiety," 117,
    157

perversion, 39–40
Ping-Pong effect, 172
Planned Parenthood, 99, 175,
    176
"playing doctor," 53
Pleasure Bond, The (Masters
    and Johnson), 19
pornography, 16, 49–50, 138–
    141
    usefulness of, 33–34, 139
pregnancy:
    in adolescence, 43, 53, 89,
        94–95, 96, 98, 103–4, 116,
        147
    children's questions about,
        80–85
    as health threat, 116
    options during, 98–99
    risk of, 42, 94–95, 123, 161–
        162
    statistics on, 89
    STDs and, 168, 170, 171
    unplanned, in Scandinavia,
        63
privacy:
    in adolescence, 104, 186
    as concept, 46, 82, 120
    of genitals, 48–49, 51–52, 53,
        78, 84
    parent–child discussions vs.,
        26, 75, 104, 114, 180
promiscuity, 27, 93, 128–29
prostitution, 84, 104, 119, 132
puberty, onset of, 94
pubic lice, 173
punishment:
    corporal, 16
    for masturbation, 118
    toilet-training and, 72
    withdrawal of love as, 22

rape, 31, 41, 119, 140
    acquaintance, 152n
    fantasies about, 32, 142
    statutory, 98–99
refractory period, 157
rejection, 22, 119

religion:
    decline of, 17, 94
    differences of, within mar-
        riage, 151
    secular humanism vs., 17, 62
    values of, 15–17, 120
Religious Values, and Peak
    Experiences (Maslow), 17
repression, 37
retardation, 188, 189
rewards, importance of, 24–25
rhythm method, 162
rock music, influence of, 14, 91,
    108
role playing, 38
romance novels, 124
Roosevelt, Eleanor, 96
Roots (Haley), 200
Roper poll (1983), 210
runaways, 103–4

sadism, 32, 33, 39, 40
Sanger, Margaret, 195
scabies, 173, 178
Scandinavia, sexuality in, 63–64,
    139–41
Schlesinger, Arthur, Jr., 20
Second Stage, The (Friedan),
    193
secular humanism, 17, 62
"self-abuse," "self-pleasuring,"
    119
self-acceptance, 146
self-esteem:
    defined, 23
    importance of, 20, 21
    in infants, 24
    low, 26–27, 31, 126, 146, 184
    promotion of, 22–28, 61, 98,
        128
    sex and, 27, 31, 111, 129,
        150
    in toddlers, 24–25
Selye, Hans, 23
sex:
    anal, 39, 155, 173
    compulsive, 129, 153

defined, 10
immature, 40
immoral, 40–41
irresponsible, 96
love vs., 19–20, 62, 99, 111,
    123, 145, 147, 148
normal, 31–32, 153, 158
oral, 39, 155, 157, 173
"quantification" of, 29
self-esteem and, 27, 31, 111,
    129, 150
sexuality vs., 10
as sin, 17
sublimation or repression of,
    37
sex crimes, 63, 118–19, 139
    see also molestation; rape
Sex for Christians (Smedes),
    143
sexism, 61, 123, 141, 154, 193,
    197
sex stereotyping, 41, 51, 73–
    74, 133, 193, 197
sexual abuse, *see* molestation
sexual arousal, 33, 44
sexual desire, 38, 142–43, 154,
    156
sexual harassment, 41
sexual intercourse:
    in adolescence, 13, 43, 53,
        88–89, 91–92, 93, 102–3,
        147
    child's observation of, 46
    evaluation of, 29–31, 35, 41,
        96–97, 101–2, 151
    extramarital, 13
    first experiences of, 41, 88–
        89, 92, 93, 102, 116–17,
        147, 151–52, 157
    frequency of, 29–30, 155
    informed consent for, 98–99
    masturbation as alternative
        to, 38, 100–101
    motivation for, 102
    in parents' home, 107
    premarital, 13, 29, 64, 103,
        107

in young adulthood, 53–54,
    102
sexuality:
    adult, 29–41
    defined, 10
    in Denmark, 63, 139
    disabilities and, 96, 117,
        183–89
    dysfunctional, 38
    of elderly, 201–2
    infantile, 71–74
    normal, 31–32, 153, 158
    orgasms vs., 20
    repression of, 37
    sex vs., 10
sexuality education:
    for disabled persons, 189–90
    distorted, sources of, 90–91
    goals and guidelines for, 59,
        64–65, 210–11
    at home, 42–54, 70, 92
    morality and, 205–11
    moral vs. moralistic, 58
    public support of, 55, 57
        59–60
    questions about, 47–54
    in Scandinavia, 63
    in schools, 54, 55–67, 89
    statistics on, 55
    in Sweden, 63–64, 140–41
    teacher's role in, 58, 60
*Sexual Morality: A Catholic
    Perspective* (Keane), 120
sexual preference, 32
    see also homosexuality
sexual revolution, 14, 128
    characteristics of, 19–20
shigellosis, 173
Siddhartha (Hesse), 107
SIECUS (Sex Information and
    Education Council of the
    United States), 57, 60
Silent Children, The (Sanford),
    79
statutory rape, 98–99
STDs (sexually transmitted dis-
    eases), 162–63, 165–78

STDs (cont.)
  decline of, in Scandinavia, 63
  homosexuality and, 173–74
  ignorance about, 43, 165
  pregnancy and, 168, 170, 171
  rise of, 13, 43, 166
  statistics on, 43, 165–66
  sterility caused by, 147, 164,
    168, 170, 172
  symptoms of, 43, 123, 174–
    175, 178
  in young adulthood, 166
  see also specific diseases
steady dating, 127–28
Stein, Benjamin, 14
sterility, 161, 163–64, 188
  STD as cause of, 147, 164,
    168, 170, 172
Strick, Lisa, 71
Strong Kids, Safe Kids
  (Winkler), 52
sublimation, 37
suicide, 104
Sweden, sexuality education in,
  63–64, 140–41
syphilis, 166, 167–68, 173, 178

teenagers, 88–164
  advice for, 111
  black, 100
  books for, 66, 104, 108, 110,
    124
  disabled, 96, 117, 185–87
  letters from, 108–11
  mature, 97, 148
  pornography read by, 34,
    138–41
  questions asked by, 52–53,
    89–90, 144–64
  rights of, 152
  self-images of, 95
  virgin vs. nonvirgin, 56
  see also adolescence; boys;
    girls
television, 190
  influence of, 14, 19, 20, 75,
    90–91, 124

violence on, 91, 140
Time, 166
Tobacco Road (Caldwell), 140
toddlers, self-esteem in, 24–25
toilet-training, 24, 72
"tomboyishness," 73
transvestism, 73
trichomonas vaginalis, 172, 178
trust, development of, 24, 25
TV Guide, 14
twins, 86

urethra, 170
urethritis, nongonococcal
    (NGU), 166, 169–70,
    172, 178

vagina, size of, 36–37, 155
vaginitis, 171, 172, 178
Values Education Commission,
    208–10
vasectomy, 161, 188
VD Hotline, 175
venereal disease, see STDs
venereal warts, 173, 178
violence:
  domestic, 76–77, 99, 192–93
  on television, 91, 139
Virginia Department of Health
    and Education, 58–59
virginity, 56, 151–52
voyeurism, 39, 40

Wachter, Oralee, 152
weaning, 24
wet dreams, 34, 79–80, 86–87
Whitaker, Carl, 199
"Winning the Battle for Sex
    Education" (Dickman),
    60
Woman's Day, 71
women:
  battered, 193
  desire in, 154
  hygiene for, 171
  insecurity of, 36–37, 41

masturbation by, 119–20,
155, 156
orgasms of, 34, 35–36, 41,
154–55
preorgasmic, 119–20, 154–55,
156
sexual dreams of, 34
sexual harassment of, 41
women's liberation, 34, 154,
191, 199

young adults, young adulthood:
questions asked by, 144–64
sexual intercourse in, 53–54,
102
STDs in, 166
Your Child's Self-Esteem
(Briggs), 26
You Would If You Loved Me
(S. Gordon), 108, 110,
149n